Breaking Down Silos for Equity, Diversity, and Inclusion (EDI)

Breaking Down Silos for Equity, Diversity, and Inclusion (EDI)

Teaching and Collaboration across Disciplines

Stephanie Burrell Storms,
Sarah K. Donovan, and
Theodora P. Williams

ROWMAN & LITTLEFIELD
Lanham • Boulder • New York • London

Published by Rowman & Littlefield
An imprint of The Rowman & Littlefield Publishing Group, Inc.
4501 Forbes Boulevard, Suite 200, Lanham, Maryland 20706
www.rowman.com

6 Tinworth Street, London SE11 5AL, United Kingdom

British Library Cataloguing in Publication Information Available

Library of Congress Cataloging-in-Publication Data

Names: Burrell Storms, Stephanie L., author. | Donovan, Sarah K., 1973- author. |
    Williams, Theodora P., 1944- author.
Title: Breaking down silos for equity, diversity, and inclusion (EDI) : teaching and
    collaboration across disciplines / Stephanie L. Burrell Storms, Sarah K. Donovan,
    Theodora P. Williams.
Description: Lanham : Rowman & Littlefield, [2020] | Includes bibliographical
    references.
Identifiers: LCCN 2019050380 (print) | LCCN 2019050381 (ebook) | ISBN
    9781475843354 (cloth) | ISBN 9781475843378 (epub) | ISBN 9781475843361
    (paperback)
Subjects: LCSH: Education—Marketing. | Schools—Marketing. | Educational
    equalization. | Multicultural education—Study and teaching. | Inclusive education—
    Study and teaching.
Classification: LCC LB2847 .B87 2020 (print) | LCC LB2847 (ebook) | DDC
    379.2/6—dc23
LC record available at https://lccn.loc.gov/2019050380
LC ebook record available at https://lccn.loc.gov/2019050381

♾™ The paper used in this publication meets the minimum requirements of
American National Standard for Information Sciences—Permanence of Paper
for Printed Library Materials, ANSI/NISO Z39.48-1992.

Contents

Foreword   vii
  Betty Overton

Preface   xi
  Stephanie L. Burrell Storms, Sarah K. Donovan, and
  Theodora P. Williams

Introduction   1
  Stephanie L. Burrell Storms, Sarah K. Donovan, and
  Theodora P. Williams

PART I: FACULTY COLLABORATION

1 Breaking Down Silos: Teaching for Equity, Diversity, and
       Inclusion Across Disciplines in Higher Education   7
       Erica E. Hartwell, Kirsten Cole, Sarah K. Donovan, Ruth L. Greene,
       Stephanie L. Burrell Storms, and Theodora P. Williams

2 Collaborative Teaching as Learning and Action   17
       Kristie A. Ford and Sarah W. Goodwin

3 Enhancing EDI Initiatives through Academic and
       Student Affairs Partnerships   25
       Ophelie Rowe-Allen and Stephanie L. Burrell Storms

**PART II: CREATIVE APPROACHES TO RESISTANCE
TO EDI GOALS**

4 Teaching about Institutional Discrimination and
       Personal Responsibility   35
       Amy Eshleman, Jean Halley, and Victoria Felix

5   Managing Your Own Socio-Emotional Landscape   43
       Theodora P. Williams, Stephanie L. Burrell Storms, and
       Sarah K. Donovan

6   Fostering Inclusivity through Social Justice Education: An
       Interdisciplinary Approach   51
       Paul Carron and Charles McDaniel

PART III: INSTITUTION-WIDE INITIATIVES

7   CIRCLE: A Research Center for EDI Initiatives   61
       Angela Fink, Erin D. Solomon, and Regina F. Frey

8   Fellows Program: Training the Next Generation of
       EDI Researchers   71
       Jacqueline Rodriquez and Natoya Haskins

9   Challenging Ableism through Community-Campus Partnerships   79
       Cynthia Kerber Gowan and Nuala Boyle

PART IV: COMMUNITY ENGAGEMENT

10 A Service-Learning Approach to Equity, Diversity, and Inclusion 91
       Ryan Colwell and Jessica Baldizon

11 Using Interdisciplinary Intersections to Promote Equity,
       Diversity, and Inclusion   101
       Sarah K. Donovan and Margarita Sánchez

PART V: FIRST-PERSON NARRATIVE

12 The Personal as Transformative in the Liberal Arts Classroom   111
       Heather Finch, Shelby Longard, and Amy Hodges Hamilton

13 We Are All in This Class:
       Digital Storytelling in the EDI Classroom   119
       Alex Miller and Theo Calhoun

About the Authors   127

Foreword

Betty Overton

Equity, diversity, and inclusion (EDI) loom large as areas of focus on college campuses today. While some still treat the term (in its varied forms: DEI, D&I, etc.) as only a short hand for what they call "diversity work," many faculty and administrators embrace the idea that EDI represents a larger goal than *just* diversifying the campus. For many of us engaged in this work, EDI is about transforming higher education into its best self. The three concepts—equity (appropriate access and opportunity), diversity (the presence of difference), and inclusion (difference valued, welcomed, and meaningfully engaged)—in their separate meanings and in their collective usage constitute strategies that are essentially about changing the ways we and our institutions work. On our campuses we are diversifying—students, faculty, staff and administrators, and, thankfully, the demographics of race, ethnicity, age, ableism, economic status, gender, sexual orientation, and other identifiers are much more visible and embraced than in the past. But for many, including the authors represented in this book series, involvement in EDI encompasses this growing diversity and a fundamental revisioning of the teaching-learning process that brings greater inclusion and equity. Moving well beyond the University of Michigan's historic court case assertion of the educational benefits of diversity, EDI is no longer a worthy but ancillary addition to the teaching, research, and service required by institutions. At the heart of EDI is this reconceptualizing of the way we approach our students, their learning, and their lived experiences of higher education. This new book, *Breaking Down Silos for Equity, Diversity, and Inclusion (EDI): Teaching and Collaboration Across Disciplines* is a glimpse into this reconceptualization. Evident in the work of the assembled authors is a picture of EDI as a process that starts with personal examination and reflection of our historic assumptions and attitudes and continues with consideration of professional commitments to unlearning or perhaps relearning what it means to teach or educate.

This book connects well to our work at the National Forum on Higher Education for the Public Good, and more recently the New Leadership Academy (NLA) at the University of Michigan. Our own work has uncovered a myriad of motivations, objectives, strategies, and outcomes for EDI. What we have learned is that this work is demanding, requiring serious "head and heart" effort; and it is messy, in that there are no quick solutions because we all enter our EDI involvement from different levels of awareness, understanding, commitment, and readiness for action. What we have also learned at the National Forum is that pushing beyond the edges of our understandings in EDI requires a willingness to take the tools of our disciplines, interlace them with interdisciplinary perspectives, and test them through ongoing feedback and dialogue with colleagues and students. The more faculty, staff, and administrators step into this space and begin to address the challenges, the more we learn. And the more we gain awareness, knowledge, and skills to work together, the better prepared we are to translate goals and intentions into classroom and cocurricular practices that support successful outcomes for students, especially those students for whom success has not always come easy.

With this book and its companion in the series, we now have another resource to help us. *Breaking Down Silos for Equity, Diversity, and Inclusion (EDI): Teaching and Collaboration Across Disciplines* reminds me of the best of our professional conferences, when we are intensely and honestly sharing about the issues that really matter to our work in EDI. Grounded in good research and practical experience, the book chapters feel like mini conference sessions presented from the perspective of those who are in the trenches every day, and what we hear from these authors is their dialogue with each other about their experimentation, learning, and glimpses of success. This publication permits us to think about how we move from conceptualization of ideas about EDI to concrete ways of acting on our convictions.

There are three unique features of the book. First, the editors of the series were intent on bringing together faculty and administrators thinking and working collaboratively on EDI issues. This companionable work serves as an example of the type of collective effort that can prove fruitful on campuses. The notion of getting out of our silos as isolated scholar-teachers or misunderstood administrators is healthy and needed to advance innovation. Second, the work shared in this volume spans disciplinary boundaries. While we continue to need close examinations of how disciplines, our usual home base, incorporate EDI, we understand that much of what we teach and what students learn takes places at the intersection of disciplines, so it is refreshing to see this interdisciplinary focus among the authors. Third, many of the chapters take us beyond the classroom and the campus and into community. This is perhaps one of the best features of the book. EDI is about us—our work in the academy—but not all about us, because what we must impress upon our students is that EDI is ultimately lived out in community. So, this effort to consciously link campus and community, not always an easy task, is laudable.

In reading this book as in attending stimulating conference sessions, you come away with a lot—ideas, clarifications, references, resources, examples, questions, motivation,M and maybe even inspiration. This last may be especially important, because those of us engaged in EDI work know how frustrating it can be as we see ourselves and our institutions take three steps forward on one day only to take two back on another. So, we are constantly in need of inspiration to move us forward.

I am so glad the editors undertook this project. I foresee the publication helping a lot of us to grow bolder in our work, buoyed in our knowledge that others too are breaking down the silos in EDI.

Betty Overton
National Forum on Higher Education for the Public Good
University of Michigan

Preface

Stephanie L. Burrell Storms, Sarah K. Donovan, and Theodora P. Williams

What does it mean to be an educator in the twenty-first century? In the summer of 2016, this question was explored by the editors of this book in a Faculty Resource Network seminar on equity, diversity, and inclusion (EDI) at New York University.

What began as an open and honest conversation about EDI developed first into a cross-discipline collaboration—and, ultimately, a published article—between six conference participants (Hartwell et al., 2017) and then into an expanded project across more disciplines in this book and its companion text, *Teaching through Challenges for Equity, Diversity, and Inclusion (EDI)*.

In these years of collaboration with each other, and with faculty across disciplines and institutions, we learned about the conflicting messages in higher education surrounding EDI. Traditionally, professors have been responsible for teaching and scholarship within their own disciplines as well as service to their institution. And while institutions and professors say that EDI goals are important, such goals have typically been seen as something to add onto many disciplines or administrative agendas rather than as integral to them.

Thus, EDI goals have been either an effort to be managed by the administration, or as something professors could choose—or not—to include in their teaching, research, or service to the university.

As more students from diverse backgrounds gain access to higher education and scholars have established the importance of a curriculum that reflects diverse perspectives (Association of American Colleges and Universities, 2015), faculty members and administrators are compelled to adjust to this new reality and reflect on what it means to the academy.

Further, students and their parents are demanding a more interactive experience in higher education. Therefore, by choice or not, faculty increasingly find themselves in the role of advisor and mentor, facilitator, scholar, academic citizen, and community member. Administrators and staff are also increasingly called upon to mentor and offer classroom instruction to students with regard to EDI.

It is this milieu that inspired this book and its companion text, *Teaching Through Challenges for Equity, Diversity, and Inclusion (EDI)*. Chapters in these books are written by faculty and administrators for educators who value the goals of EDI and who seek an intellectual community to help them develop their practice.

Each chapter is designed for use by instructors and administrators in higher education who believe that the goals of EDI should be integrated into the classroom experience and the college experience as a whole and not be isolated units in an otherwise unchallenged, culturally monolithic curriculum.

REFERENCES

Association of American Colleges and Universities. (2015). Committing to equity and inclusive excellence: A campus guide for self-study and planning. Retrieved from https://www.aacu.org/sites/default/files/CommittingtoEquityInclusiveExcellence.pdf.

Hartwell, E., Cole, K., Donohue, S., Greene, R., Burrell Storms, S., and Williams, T. (2017). Breaking down silos: Teaching equity, diversity, and inclusion across the disciplines, *Humboldt Journal of Social Relations*, 1(39), 143–62.

Introduction

Stephanie L. Burrell Storms, Sarah K. Donovan, and Theodora P. Williams

Chapters in this book include practical and practiced teaching strategies that have been successful in various courses—from education, to business, to philosophy, and the sciences. There is a disctinct focus on supporting faculty and administrators to educate students from diverse populations so that those students can develop cultural awareness and become sensitive to, and challenge, their own biases as they enter their professional lives.

To promote EDI-relevant goals, the chapters in this book are grouped around five central themes that challenge the structure of a traditional classroom to promote EDI-relevant goals: faculty collaboration; creative approaches to faculty and student resistance to EDI goals; institution-wide initiatives; community engagement; and the use of first-person autobiography and storytelling in the classroom.

Chapters one, two, and three address, from distinct perspectives, how faculty collaboration promotes EDI goals. In chapter one, authors Hartwell, Cole, Donovan, Greene, Burrell Storms, and Williams discuss a collaboration between faculty members from diverse disciplines that explored interdisciplinary EDI strategies both in the classroom and in community-based projects. This collaboration and chapter was the catalyst for this current book.

In chapter two, Ford and Goodwin analyze the challenges, tensions, and opportunities in a cornerstone collaborative-teaching course within an Intergroup Relations program. The authors identify and focus on three processes that were essential to their dialogue-based course: (1) naming the power dynamics; (2) building trust/overcoming fear of imperfection; and (3) modeling self-discovery and vulnerability.

Rowe-Allen and Burrell Storms, in chapter three, expand the scope of collaboration to discuss how partnerships between academic and student affairs are essential to the creation of successful student-learning environments that emphasize EDI. Rowe-Allen, from student affairs, and Burrell Storms, from an academic teacher preparation program, provide two examples that illustrate how EDI can be enhanced through collaboration.

Chapters four, five, and six take as their starting point acknowledgment of how students and faculty may resist the goals of EDI. They then offer creative approaches for addressing resistance. In chapter four, authors Eshleman, Halley, and Felix explore two approaches to effective teaching for EDI. The first approach focuses on evidence of institutional discrimination before addressing personal responsibility, while the second requires a sustained focus on discrimination despite predictable initial resistance from students.

While the authors recognize that both approaches increase the potential for students to become powerful upstanders who affect peers beyond the classroom, they also demonstrate that the first approach is a path of less resistance.

Williams, Burrell Storms, and Donovan puzzle through what makes faculty resist EDI topics in the classroom in chapter five. They hone in on the socio-emotional experience of the faculty member when the conversations get uncomfortable in order to explore what triggers faculty and how they can manage their own emotions in those moments.

In chapter six, Carron and McDaniel describe how they team-taught a two-semester social justice course to a predominantly white, economically privileged, and insular community. Their chapter is ideal for professors who find that they must justify the need for EDI to their students before they can even begin to teach it. These authors provide ideas that can be incorporated into other disciplines and courses so that students understand the importance of breaking down barriers that prevent inclusivity.

Chapters seven, eight, and nine utilize three distinct institution-wide initiatives that promote EDI across campuses. In chapter seven, Fink, Solomon, and Frey describe a university-supported research center—its mission and methods—to highlight the ways in which EDI initiatives can be instrumental in creating and forging connections among faculty, administrators, and staff. By discussing the history of the research center at their university, the authors provide a look at some of the challenges faced and the steps taken to overcome them.

In chapter eight, Rodriguez and Haskins address the need for mentorship and training for graduate students across disciplines in EDI research. They draw on the example of their institution, which secured a Mellon Foundation Grant to establish a graduate Fellows Program to mentor graduate students as they develop research areas related to EDI. As this chapter discusses the need for such programs, it also addresses how these programs can be replicated.

Gowan and Boyle discuss in chapter nine a comprehensive model at their institution for a campus-based community partnership that challenges the lack of education opportunities for individuals who may have been labeled intellectually or developmentally disabled but are better described as diverse or differently abled. The goal of the program is not only to empower the students who participate but also to expand the definition of diversity on a college campus to include ability.

Authors Colwell and Baldizon, in chapter ten, and Donovan and Sánchez, in chapter eleven, discuss how effective community engagement can promote EDI goals. Colwell and Baldizon discuss how four critical service-learning practices empowered university and community partners to address EDI issues.

While applicable across disciplines, they draw on a university literacy methods course and the diverse, urban school in which the courses were embedded as a service-learning component. The chapter focuses on: (1) relationship-building; (2) challenging preexisting ideas and beliefs; (3) blending content and experiential learning opportunities; and (4) engaging in assessment, reflection, and goal setting.

Donovan and Sánchez offer strategies and practices for utilizing experiential learning to integrate disciplines while embedding EDI into the curriculum. Utilizing a learning community that combines the disciplines of Spanish and philosophy as their primary example, the authors identify and describe four general strategies and practices to advance EDI goals. They also indicate how these strategies and practices are applicable across or between many disciplines.

Chapters twelve and thirteen share the common theme of utilizing the first-person narrative to disrupt the traditional classroom and promote EDI goals. In chapter twelve, Finch, Longard, and Hamilton discuss how autobiography can be a powerful tool for educators as they guide students through classroom discussions about EDI.

In the context of interdisciplinary teaching and writing, they demonstrate how autobiography can open up spaces to empower students and teachers alike. They maintain that educators developing "conscious vulnerability" with autobiography enrich how students approach EDI in the classroom.

Miller and Calhoun, a professor and a student, respectively, provide a case study in chapter thirteen that combines storytelling and historically focused scholarship to cultivate equitable, diverse, and inclusive classrooms. Their discussion further explores the importance of student voices and lived experiences in the dominant academic discourse, offering techniques designed to remove the barriers between students and faculty.

While all of the chapters discuss different aspects of EDI in the higher education classroom with specific disciplines in mind, the strategies, activities, and insights are broadly applicable across disciplines and institutions. The goal of writing for multiple disciplines is to emphasize that educators should move beyond identifying EDI goals as belonging to select specializations within specific disciplines such as education or sociology. To serve twenty-first-century students and prepare them to be successful in an increasingly diverse world, EDI goals are within the purview of all disciplines.

Part I

FACULTY COLLABORATION

Chapter One

Breaking Down Silos: Teaching for Equity, Diversity, and Inclusion Across Disciplines in Higher Education

Erica E. Hartwell, Kirsten Cole, Sarah K. Donovan, Ruth L. Greene, Stephanie L. Burrell Storms, and Theodora P. Williams

Across disciplines, instructors in higher education incorporate issues of equity, diversity, and inclusion (EDI) into their courses. This chapter uses the widely accepted learning objectives of awareness, knowledge, and skill (Adams, 2016; Fuentes, Chanthongthi, and Rios, 2010; Mayhew and Fernández, 2007; Sue, 2001; Sue, Arredondo, and McDavis, 1992) and the additional objective of action (Burrell Storms, 2012; Iverson, 2012) to introduce teaching strategies, classroom activities, and both service-learning and community-based projects that can be adapted across disciplines to meet EDI-focused learning objectives.

AWARENESS

To acquire knowledge, develop skills, and engage in action regarding EDI, students must first develop an awareness of their own social and cultural identities, values, and biases. This type of learning occurs in the affective domain, through the sharing of personal stories among the instructor, classmates, and community members. Students may experience this as unorthodox or even intimidating, but three practices create a safe and effective learning environment: (1) building awareness early in the course, (2) developing an awareness of self before learning about others, and (3) debriefing exercises to help students make connections.

Building Awareness Early

Early introduction of activities with the objective of developing self-awareness serves a dual purpose of providing an opportunity for establishing norms for acceptable interaction student-to-student and teacher-to-student, and for the instructor to more quickly develop insights into students' preferred learning styles. One sample activity is the cultural chest activity.

Introducing a cultural chest activity (Williams, 2010) on the first day of class sets the expectation that students will engage in self-discovery in a course. For this activity, students select three objects that describe an aspect of their social identity and place these objects in a bag or box. Instructors first share their own cultural chest, modeling self-awareness and an openness to self-reflection. Students then decorate the outside of the box or bag with images that demonstrate how they believe others see them. In short presentations, students share their boxes, and classmates take notes for a debriefing session at the end of all presentations.

Developing Awareness of Self

Students and instructors of EDI courses often make the mistake of prioritizing cultural competence, the accumulation of knowledge about cultures other than their own, over cultural humility, a self-reflexive process of examining biases and seeking to understand each person's context (Rincón, 2009; Tervalon and Murray-Garcia, 1998).

Students belonging to social groups that have historically been privileged often believe that culture belongs to others. To avoid this mistake, EDI instructors should emphasize and model for their students the importance of developing self-awareness before attempting to learn about others. A cultural genogram is one such activity that addresses this goal.

A cultural genogram (Hardy and Lazsloffy, 1995) is a visual history of a family's cultural background, including gender, race, ethnicity, nationality, class, religion, sexual orientation, and ability. Completing a cultural genogram can increase student awareness of their own cultural identities while also increasing sensitivity towards differences in the culture of others.

In one marriage and family therapy course, the instructor has students create a three-generation cultural genogram and write a paper reflecting on how their family background might impact their clinical work. This activity reveals complex life experiences and social identities to individuals in a seemingly homogenous classroom.

Debriefing to Make Connections

Debriefing is especially important after activities that challenge students' personal beliefs, values, or worldview. For example, following the cultural chest activity, one instructor from education asks questions such as, "What were some of the commonalities and/or differences you heard from the stories your classmates shared? Whose voices are missing? How might you use this activity in your own classrooms?"

If students can identify patterns that emerge during an activity like this, they can often relate these patterns to the rest of society. A case in point is that white students tend to share an object that signifies their ethnicity but not their race. Students of color are more likely to share an object that signifies their race but not their social class. These patterns can be used to further discussions about EDI within numerous disciplines as well as within society.

KNOWLEDGE

While instructors of EDI must provide their students with content knowledge specific to their discipline, three essential strategies for increasing student knowledge regarding EDI are the following: (1) activate prior knowledge, (2) connect learning to the discipline, and (3) provide tools for continued learning.

Activate Prior Knowledge

One way an education instructor activates students' prior knowledge of their own identities is by first framing the conversation using writing about white privilege by authors such as McIntosh (1988). The instructor then asks students to create an "Identity Wheel" (Griffin, 2007) through which they identify their social group identities and their social statuses (privileged or nondominant). Afterward, students discuss questions such as, "Which identities do you think about most often and least often? Which identities were difficult for you to identify and why?"

The instructor builds on these understandings with an activity called "Common Ground" (Bell, Joshi, and Zúñiga, 2007) in which students stand in a circle in silence. The instructor calls out a list of different privileges, and students step inside the circle if the example applies to their life experience.

This pair of activities helps to make invisible advantages visible, but these hands-on, experiential learning activities can feel risky. A simple way to debrief is to give students the opportunity to write for three to five minutes after the activity, followed by a class discussion about what they experienced.

Connect Learning to Discipline

Students sometimes have difficulty seeing how EDI issues connect back to their field of study, discipline, or intended profession. Instructors can bring

EDI concepts to life for students through interdisciplinary courses, service learning, and community-based partnerships.

In one example, a philosophy professor teaches a course that introduces traditional Western ethical theories in a learning community with a professor from a different discipline, such as documentary filmmaking or Spanish. Students and instructors weave together philosophical discussions of obligation with information about immigration, education, and filmmaking. Community-based projects include documentary film work or after-school tutoring at local immigrant centers.

Drawing on the knowledge base and methodology of other disciplines and the community-based project, students explore theoretical questions in the concrete, such as the following: "Do we have an obligation to people that we do not know?"; "How does our relationship with other people influence our own self-perception and identity?"; and "How does our ability to communicate (specifically, with language) affect how we treat other people?"

In disciplines that are less abstract, community-based projects are a clear fit for introducing EDI themes. For example, an educational psychology instructor engages students in a community-based project where they gain knowledge from readings and training in order to serve as volunteers for an organization that seeks to eliminate health disparities that affect racial, ethnic, and other at-risk populations.

In addition to providing support to participants and session speakers, students participate in a breakout session with young adults that focuses on health issues; it is an opportunity for students to apply discipline-specific knowledge about child and youth development to an equity issue in a community setting.

Provide Tools for Continued Learning

When learning about systematic inequities, oppression, and privilege, students can often feel overwhelmed and paralyzed. Students can benefit from simple, manageable tools. One instructor of marriage and family therapy uses a three-step consciousness-raising model to help students deconstruct oppressive behaviors, structures, or institutions: (1) What is the bias, assumption, or type of oppression present?; (2) What context, history, or narrative can help you understand this bias?; and (3) What can you or others do instead?

For example, if a student comments that gender roles for young girls have been expanding while young boys who are into "girl" things continue to be ridiculed, the instructor guides the class to unpack this inequity using the three-step model. First, identify assumptions underlying this double standard.

Secondly, name the societal structure that reinforces the assumptions (in this case, patriarchy). Finally, discuss what each person could do differently.

This three-step consciousness model is introduced early in the course when the instructor explains that we all have biases and assumptions. Students often feel upset that they have potentially harmful or oppressive biases. The role of the instructor is to help them to unpack their biases, to understand where they came from, and to take responsibility for making a change.

SKILLS

In addition to awareness and knowledge, students need to develop behaviors necessary to translate awareness and knowledge into practice. Given that EDI skills center on behavior, communication, and engagement with people different from ourselves, instructor-modeling and student activities can be used to teach both communication and interpersonal skills.

Communication Skills

Communication skills include the ability to both use effective and appropriate language and to engage in active listening. Instructors model effective and appropriate language given current social norms, one's own identity, and one's professional role. Students are encouraged to ask questions when proper terms are unknown and to learn to challenge unexamined normative frameworks.

One effective sample assignment that accomplishes these goals is from an education course in which students select current instructional materials in their teaching area and write a paper for presentation that describes the material, analyzes it for how it portrays social groups positively, negatively, or not at all, and suggests ways they could supplement or use it in their own classrooms.

Detecting this type of bias in instructional materials is a critical skill for current and future teachers not only as they make pedagogical choices but also as they educate others about the problem of bias. Similar assignments could be developed in various disciplines with the same goals.

Engaged active listening is an important and related communication skill. A simple way for an instructor to model this skill is to reflect back to the students what has been heard. Instructors can go further and create a collaborative classroom environment where the hierarchy of instructor and student is flattened to a degree. Instructors can introduce students to this environment by inviting them to challenge the instructor's viewpoint or to help the instructor identify their own bias. This creates opportunities to model openness to hearing and processing feedback.

Interpersonal Skills

The interpersonal skills necessary for EDI work include the following: (1) being able to collaborate within and across difference, (2) developing empathy, and (3) managing discomfort. Classroom environments present many opportunities for collaborating within and across differences, and the instructor models this type of interaction.

For example, an instructor can ask students to co-create in-class discussion guidelines. When students offer typical responses such as, "Keep an open mind" or "Don't be biased," this allows the instructor to introduce questions such as, "What is bias? Where does bias come from? Is it possible to be unbiased?" With this added layer of nuance, students can work collaboratively to develop agreed-upon guidelines, such as: "Be aware of your biases, and work to overcome them."

Developing empathy is also central to EDI work, and an example from a marriage and family therapy course provides strategies applicable across disciplines. In this course, the instructor collaborates with the university's summer-writing institute to create an intergroup dialogue that brings together people from different social identity groups. They develop empathy as they build nonhierarchical relationships, engage in cross-cultural communication, and discover similarities and differences across their experiences (Nagda and Gurin, 2007).

Discomfort can arise when students are asked to challenge concepts and biases (conscious or unconscious). Managing discomfort is central to both processing and dismantling bias. Instructors are most effective when they provide a safe, agenda-free space for students to wrestle with new perspectives, such as informal in-class writing prior to discussion.

More often, modeling how to manage discomfort happens spontaneously. In one education course, when discussing *In Our Mothers' House* (Polacco 2009), a children's book that centers on a family with two mothers, two students reflected to each other that the story seemed "a little weird" to them. The instructor acknowledged their discomfort and asked if the class could think of more inclusive language to describe their feelings. The class agreed that the phrase, "I realize this is pushing me out of my comfort zone," expressed discomfort and made space for everyone. Instructors can use similar classroom moments to encourage students to identify and process discomfort.

ACTION

Awareness, knowledge, and skills are all essential but have more meaning for students when they are also translated into concrete projects. What follows are examples of how instructors can construct highly adaptable off-campus projects and on-campus activities from multiple disciplines that present students with opportunities for action. The focus of these projects and activities is on either identifying EDI issues in the real world or developing solutions and recommendations to promote EDI.

Identifying EDI in the Real World

Before students can engage in social action, they must be able to recognize what injustice looks like in the real world. One sample project that helps students identify EDI with an eye towards action involves teacher-education students assessing social institutions' support of social justice education. Teams of three to four students conduct interviews, observations, and document analysis to understand what schools (or other social institutions) do or do not do to prepare students to live in an increasingly diverse society. Through this assignment, students see firsthand how policies and practices privilege some and marginalize others.

In a second sample project, business students, working in small groups, use critical thinking skills and their knowledge of business concepts to identify various socioeconomic differences and cultural norms that have been created by the manufacturing economy in an inner city. As they note the current suburban location of most entry-level manufacturing jobs now, students quickly begin to recognize and understand inherent problems with equity and access to services and opportunity. These discoveries are shared in a large group debriefing session.

Developing Solutions or Recommendations to Promote EDI

Students who can recognize acts of social injustice in their communities or relationships are often motivated to be agents of change but are not sure where to start. To help them understand how they can take action within their professional sphere, a marriage and family therapy instructor uses an activity called an "Access and Inclusion Photo Hunt."

For this assignment, the entire class takes a field trip to the department's on-campus marriage and family therapy clinic. In groups, students document the strengths and weaknesses of access and inclusion with photos. They also consult with the instructor and a staff member from the disability services office who answer student questions about things such as session fees and door width requirements for wheelchair access. The opportunity to brainstorm solutions and ways to increase inclusion within their own professional practice settings puts students in a better position to be change agents and advocates in their future professions.

CONCLUSION

This chapter introduces and utilizes the four learning objectives of awareness, knowledge, skills, and action to highlight a range of pedagogical strategies that foster EDI in the classroom. Further, many of the approaches can be translated across disciplinary silos so that instructors can increase the number of courses within their disciplines that reflect the values of EDI.

NOTE

A longer version of this chapter was published in the *Humboldt Journal of Social Relations*: Hartwell, E., Cole, K., Donohue, S., Greene, R., Burrell Storms, S., and Williams, T. (2017). Breaking down silos: Teaching equity, diversity, and inclusion across the disciplines, *Humboldt Journal of Social Relations*, 1(39), 143–62.

REFERENCES

Adams, M. (2016). Pedagogical foundations for social justice education. In M. Adams, L. A. Bell, D. J. Goodman, and K. Y. Joshi (Eds.), *Teaching for Diversity and Social Justice* (3rd ed.) (pp. 27–54). New York: Routledge.

Bell, L. A., Joshi, K. Y., and Zúñiga, X. (2007). Racism, immigration, and globalization curriculum design. In M. Adams, L. A. Bell, and P. Griffin (Eds.), *Teaching for Diversity and Social Justice* (2nd ed.) (pp. 145–66). New York: Routledge.

Burrell Storms, S. (2012). Preparing students for social action in a social justice education course: What works? *Equity & Excellence in Education*, 45(4), 547–60.

Fuentes, R., Chanthongthi, L., and Rios, F. (2010). Teaching and learning social justice as an 'Intellectual Community' requirement: Pedagogical opportunities and student understandings. *Equity & Excellence in Education*, 43(3), 357–74.

Griffin, P. (2007). Introductory module 2. In M. Adams, L. A. Bell, and P. Griffin (Eds.), *Teaching for Diversity and Social Justice* (2nd ed.) (p. 64). New York: Routledge.

Hardy, K., and Laszloffy, T. A. (1995). The cultural genogram: Key to training culturally competent family therapists. *Journal of Marital and Family Therapy*, 21(3), 227–37.

Iverson, S. V. (2012). Multicultural competence for doing social justice: Expanding our awareness, knowledge, and skills. *Journal of Critical Thought and Praxis*, 1(1), Article 5.

Mayhew, M. J., and Fernández, S. D. (2007). Pedagogical practices that contribute to social justice outcomes. *Review of Higher Education*, 31, 55–80.

McIntosh, P. (1988). White privilege: Unpacking the invisible knapsack. *Race, Class, and Gender in the United States: An Integrated Study*, 4, 165–69.

Nagda, B. A., and Gurin, P. (2007). Intergroup dialogue: A critical-dialogic approach to learning about difference, inequality, and social justice. *New Directions for Teaching & Learning*, 111, 35–45.

Polacco, P. (2009). *In our mothers' house.* New York: Philomel Books.

Rincón, A. M. (2009). Practicing cultural humility. In T. Berthold, J. Miller, and A. Avila-Esparza (Eds.), *Foundations for Community Health Workers* (pp. 135–54). San Francisco: Jossey-Bass.

Sue, D. W. (2001). Multidimensional facets of cultural competence. *The Counseling Psychologist*, 29(6), 790–821.

Sue, D. W., Arredondo, P., and McDavis, R. J. (1992). Multicultural counseling competencies and standards: A call to the profession. *Journal of Counseling & Development*, 70(4), 477–86.

Tervalon, M., and Murray-Garcia, J. (1998). Cultural humility versus cultural competence: A critical distinction in defining physician training outcomes in multicultural education. *Journal of Health Care for the Poor and Underserved*, 9(2),117–25.

Williams, T. O. (2010). Cultural chest activity. In M. Adams, W. J. Blumenfeld, C. R. Castañeda, H. W. Hackman, M. L. Peters, and X. Zúñiga (Eds.), *Readings for Diversity and Social Justice* (2nd ed.) (p. 3B). New York: Routledge.

Chapter Two

Collaborative Teaching as Learning and Action

Kristie A. Ford and Sarah W. Goodwin

The chapter that follows takes as a given that there are very real challenges in collaborative, dialogue-based teaching in which both the faculty and the students come from different social identities. In particular, one course serves here as an example of the ways that awareness, knowledge, and skills must all come into play as both faculty and students navigate unanticipated and challenging situations. Even with extensive experience or scholarship in dialogue-based pedagogies, as well as a commitment to action and transformation as ultimate goals, collaborating faculty may encounter challenges that require new conceptualization and skills.

This chapter begins with an introduction to the course that is the focus of this chapter and the challenges that the faculty faced. It then turns to three pedagogical interventions that were essential to sustaining an effective dialogue-based course: (1) naming the power dynamics; (2) building trust/overcoming fear of imperfection; and (3) modeling self-discovery and vulnerability. All three processes require the co-teaching faculty to work separately in addition to working collaboratively and flexibly with the students.

THE COURSE: RACIAL IDENTITIES: THEORY AND PRAXIS

This chapter focuses on a course that is offered within the program on Intergroup Relations (IGR) at Skidmore College. A form of social justice education, IGR is a nationally recognized academic, credit-bearing program that originated at the University of Michigan in 1988 as a means of addressing racial tension and supporting student learning and competencies around conflict, communication, and social justice.

Since then, it has expanded to a number of other colleges and universities across the United States. In 2012, Skidmore College became the first to offer a minor in IGR. Under the umbrella of IGR, Intergroup Dialogue (IGD) is defined by Zúñiga, Nagda, Chesler, and Cytron (2007) as a facilitated, face-to-face encounter that aims to cultivate meaningful engagement between members of two or more social identity groups that have a history of conflict.

The components that distinguish IGD from more traditional courses include: (1) structured, small-group interactions; (2) engaged pedagogies that balance content and process knowledge; and (3) a co-learning environment led by two trained peer-facilitators (in Ford and Malaney, 2012; Nagda, Gurin, Sorensen, and Zúñiga, 2009; Zúñiga et al., 2007).

"Racial Identities: Theory and Praxis" (Racial ID) is the minor's advanced training course for students interested in facilitating race dialogues. Using the fall 2017 iteration of Racial ID as a case study, this chapter highlights collaborative teaching as a promising pedagogical practice that surfaces the challenges, tensions, and opportunities for transformation inherent in equity, diversity, and inclusion (EDI) work.

Racial ID is unique to IGR: Students apply to enroll in the course, and the enrollment is limited and balanced regarding racial identity. Half of the students self-identify as students of color and half as white students. An advanced IGR course that bridges theory (content) with its application (process), Racial ID trains undergraduate students to co-facilitate credit-bearing dialogues on race. Using the passion, awareness, skills, and knowledge (PASK) framework (Maxwell, Fisher, Thompson, and Behling, 2011, p. 44), co-instructors of differing racial identities and disciplinary backgrounds[1] model for students critical-dialogic facilitation techniques.

The training and support model for peer-facilitators centers on four components: (1) increasing facilitator knowledge of relevant theory; (2) encouraging facilitators' self-awareness; (3) building facilitator social justice pedagogy skills; and (4) developing a nuanced understanding of inter-/intragroup dynamics (Maxwell, Fisher, Thompson, and Behling, 2011; also, see Ford, 2018).

The course is structured with theoretical readings and dialogue exercises in the first half; then, working in pairs, the students plan and facilitate two *content*-based dialogues: one in class, and one outside of class. The instructors then facilitate a dialogue about the *process*, reflecting on the lesson plan, the group dynamics, and facilitation effectiveness.

Students who wish to co-facilitate one of the program's peer-led dialogue courses must complete prerequisites and then take Racial ID. These students then become both skilled in interracial dialogues and highly motivated. Both instructors, Ford and Goodwin, had taught the course repeatedly over a period of ten years.

In this iteration, there was no reason to expect the group's dynamic to be any more complicated than usual. Nonetheless, it proved difficult. Through critical self-reflection, instructor debriefing sessions, qualitative analysis of students' final papers ($n=9^2$), and course evaluations, we showcase the challenges and opportunities of collaborative teaching through an EDI lens and highlight the central challenges that are recurrent themes in the data.

THE CHALLENGES

Contrary to the instructors' expectations, the dialogues in this group had trouble getting underway. Some of the students were unusually quiet. Several students did talk quite a bit, but even they sometimes retreated into silence. When they did talk, they often stumbled. As one student noted in a course evaluation at the end, "There was usually a reserved aspect to our class, and I can recognize my own reservedness, and I am not sure how that could have been resolved."

By mid-semester, the instructors and students were actively trying to understand the group's challenges. Students further refined their reflections in the final self-reflective paper at the end of the semester. A pattern emerged there: (1) all students feared expressing emotion; (2) students of color held back; (3) white students dominated dialogues with critical self-reflections; (4) all feared being less than perfect; and (5) the awkwardness persisted. For the faculty, the challenge was, "What caused this pattern? And what steps could break the class out of it?"

A recurrent theme in the students' papers was their fear of expressing emotion or of getting out of control somehow. One student of color wrote about feeling "dread and aversion" and fearing to take risks. Others observed that white students were more likely to speak impersonally, to withhold emotions more than the students of color.

For instance, a student of color wrote that "We made too much room for the over-intellectualization of our topic and too little room for personal experience." Further, a white student wrote, "This also shows some power dynamics: White people were speaking more analytically, intellectualizing accountability, and people of color were generally speaking more emotionally and vulnerably."

The students also tended to identify withholding emotion and vulnerability with a general fear. One student of color wrote the following: "Because most of the participants in our dialogue were more reserved, it forced all of us to recognize the importance of taking risks in the dialogue and trying to model the vulnerability that we wanted to see."

Similarly, one white student wrote the following: "I...have seen through-out this class and our dialogues how the fear of saying the wrong things or gaining bad reputation can stifle a dialogue." Another white student wrote, in the final paper, "I had not realized the emotional privilege of being reserved that I attain from my race....I have to recognize that each time I refrain from partaking in a vulnerable discussion, I participate in the larger concept of white privilege."

Students related fear to a pressure many felt to be "perfect." One student wrote: "While writing this paper, I put so much pressure on myself to be per-fect. At times, I felt restrained, stuck, and could not write a word more. This is ironic because it is similar to my challenges in dialogue as a participant and facilitator this semester."

Another stated: "I am trying, however, to take more risks, and if I do make mistakes, to see them as a learning moment instead of indicative of a charac-ter flaw." They needed to let go of the pressure to be perfect and to see fear, risks, and failures as all crucial parts of the process.

Even in this experienced and mixed-race group, white dominance was a factor that the students themselves identified as a problem: as one student of color wrote, "[I]t's ironic that we had the exact opposite dynamic in class: white dominance....white students...seemed to be working through feel-ings of white guilt and confusion..." Several voluble white students tried to restrain their voices, stating, for example, "I think I'm taking up too much space."

A white student identified the negative consequence: "I struggled to use my voice to the best end this semester, only to realize that I was still using it for myself rather than to probe others..." Unfortunately, a major consequence of the white students' acute self-consciousness was a delay in the dialogue's development as they struggled to become more full participants and effective listeners.

All the challenges outlined in this chapter are not atypical in an intergroup dialogue course. Taken together, in this case, they formed a persistent nega-tive pattern that required strategic pedagogical interventions to disrupt.

PEDAGOGICAL INTERVENTIONS

To address these challenges, the instructors met weekly to debrief the group dynamics and discuss potential solutions. In the end, according to student self-reflections, three practices seemed to have the most impact on shifting the class in productive ways.

Naming Power Dynamics

First, throughout the semester, the instructors increasingly named the various power dynamics that they observed. Through Freire's (1968) work, students were reminded of the importance of finding the appropriate balance between content and process goals in hopes of establishing a brave space[3] of co-learning and reflection.

As one student of color noted: "This class has shown me the power of calling out things in the moment and the honesty and learning that can come from that." The instructors found it even more necessary than usual to adapt lesson plans in the moment to address process issues as they arose, even if it meant a complete change of plan.

The instructors, however, were slow to realize the negative impact on the class of white students' ongoing self-criticism and resulting self-absorption. That was a part of a power dynamic that could beneficially have been named sooner.

Building Trust

A brave space of learning and growth cannot be achieved without trust in the group—starting with one's co-facilitator. One of the challenges in the course, it became clear, was for the two *faculty* to build and model the kind of trusting relationship that is visible in a dialogue and invites full participation from all present.

It took some time for the instructors to find a co-facilitation mode that could be appropriately discreet while also allowing for some emotional vitality and vulnerability. As the white instructor wrote to her black colleague in the fifth week of the class:

> I have felt pretty awkward in the class so far and would like to unpack the awkwardness in hopes that you and I can help to model and establish a little more open flow in the group. My primary concern is feeling caught between carrying enough of the load that you and I actually share it, and [in contrast] being too strong a voice. After the class yesterday, several of the white students were talking about a similar challenge.

The instructor of color responded, "Yes, I do think we need to find a time...to unpack the group dynamics. They feel odd, and I want to make sure we (and the group) are successful in Racial ID."

To negotiate this, Ford and Goodwin had frequent open, honest, and difficult conversations between themselves—questioning how their own racialized positionalities affected the class. As referenced above, Goodwin, whose primary disciplinary background did not align with IGR practices, felt somewhat insecure about the course material and, therefore, relied more heavily on Ford. Ford, in turn, felt the pressure to be perfect, as she was often viewed by her co-instructor, and the students, as the IGR "expert," which was also complicated by her identity as a black woman.

Through active listening and perspective-taking, Ford and Goodwin worked through their own internal conflicts, as well as how these conflicts were surfacing within the classroom space. It was crucial for the instructors to cultivate a mutual trust and openness and to model that for the students. That process was not always easy. However, the process is ongoing because the dialogues themselves are not just theorizing about intergroup communication but practicing it, in a way that makes the classroom a permeable part of real-world identities, behaviors, and transformations (see Blanchard, 2012).

The instructors expected students in Racial ID to go through a similar process of self-discovery. A "conflict history assessment," an exercise that asked students to reflect on and share how they were socialized to engage with conflict as a child, proved to be a particularly powerful pedagogical tool for the student co-facilitator teams.

The exercise achieved two goals: it (1) built trust through mutual vulnerability and risk-taking, and (2) provided useful information about conflict styles and how they might impact co-facilitator responses in the dialogue.

In fact, several students, exemplified in the following example, reported that the conflict history assessment was a turning point in their co-facilitation relationship:

> One thing I have learned through this course and co-facilitation project is that it is important to have a close and comfortable relationship with your co-facilitator. [NAME] and I were awkward and probably overly careful with each other at first, and planning and conducting our dialogues got much easier as we got to know each other. Although it happened after our facilitations, one of the most beneficial exercises for me was when we talked about how our families managed conflict. We were able to relate and be vulnerable with each other through this exercise, and I think it has allowed us to be more open with each other since.

Modeling Vulnerability and Turning Mistakes into Teachable Moments

Finally, trust was also enhanced within the class when the instructors modeled vulnerability—sharing their personal lived experiences, highlighting their facilitation mistakes, and using these self-revelations as teachable moments.

Specifically, "dialoguing about the dialogue"—spending time after the *content* dialogue concluded to discuss the *process* of emotional engagement—allowed time for the class to unpack further how the instructors and students may have contributed to productive as well as challenging group dynamics.

More concretely, the instructors were able to demonstrate how we were all learning with, and from, each other in IGR and that mistakes, especially when dealing with social justice-related topics, are inevitable. This seemed beneficial in reassuring the student facilitators that perfection is not possible or even ideal. Quotations from a white student and student of color, respectively, highlighted this point:

> As a facilitator, there is a pressure to be a perfect model and example, but I also feel like one of the best ways to connect with people is by sharing stories of failure. The times when I have felt most comfortable with Professor Ford and Professor Goodwin are when they have shared about their struggles and how they are overcoming them, not when I see them facilitating perfectly.
>
> This class really challenged me to grow in my relationship with my own emotions, especially because I can't expect a classroom of students to share their emotions if I'm not willing to do it myself...even when we had issues in the class, it felt like the safest place to mess up, admit, and try to do better, which is an attitude that I think is integral to this [IGR] minor and to social justice in general.

CONCLUSION

Teaching is inevitably a reciprocal, co-learning process; this case study demonstrates how Ford and Goodwin learned alongside the students in unexpected ways. Even though both are experienced instructors, they found that they were still refining their own awareness, skills, and knowledge even as they applied them with a group of students who presented some challenging group dynamics.

Despite these challenges, however, the sense of connectedness exhibited in students' critical reflections in their final papers; "perfect" fives across all the numerical teaching evaluations; and the ongoing and strong working relationships developed with these students all showcase the power of dialogue as a transformative experience within EDI courses.

In sum, by collaboratively teaching an EDI course across racial identity categories, the realization that the doing and the learning are interconnected became apparent. In this way, the instructors modeled for the students, and also learned from them, how to elicit fully engaged, courageous dialogue.

NOTES

1. Ford identifies as a black woman in Sociology, and Goodwin is a white woman in English.
2. Nine of the eleven students signed the IRB approved consent form to participate in this study.
3. Rather than attempting to achieve emotional safety, brave spaces focus on the courage needed to engage in difficult dialogues (Arao and Clemens, 2013).

REFERENCES

Arao, B., and Clemens, K. (2013). From safe to brave spaces: A new way to frame dialogue around diversity and social justice. In L. M. Landreman (Ed.), *The Art of Effective Facilitation* (pp. 135–50). Sterling, VA: Stylus, Publishing, Inc.

Blanchard, K. D. (2012). Modeling lifelong learning: Collaborative teaching across disciplinary lines. *Teaching Theology & Religion*, 15(4), 338–54.

Ford, K. (2018). *Facilitating Change through Intergroup Dialogue: Social Justice Advocacy in Practice.* New York: Routledge.

Ford, K. A., and Malaney, V. K. (2012). I now harbor more pride in my race: The educational benefits of inter- and intraracial dialogues on the experiences of students of color and multiracial students. *Equity & Excellence in Education*, 45(1), 14–35. Reprinted by permission of Taylor & Francis, Ltd, http://www.tandfonline.com.

Freire, P. (1968). *Pedagogy of the Oppressed.* New York: Bloomsbury.

Maxwell, K. E., Fisher, R. B., Thompson, M. C., and Behling, C. (2011). Training peer facilitators as social justice educators. In K. E. Maxwell, R. A. Nagda, and M. C. Thompson (Eds.), *Facilitating Intergroup Dialogues: Bridging Differences, Catalyzing Change* (pp. 41–54). Sterling, VA: Stylus Publishing, Inc.

Nagda, B. A., Gurin, P., Sorensen, N., and Zúñiga, X. (2009). Evaluating intergroup dialogue: Engaging diversity for personal and social responsibility. *Diversity & Democracy*, 12(1), 1–5.

Zúñiga, X., Nagda, B. A., Chesler, M., and Cytron, A. (2007). Intergroup dialogue in higher education: Meaningful learning about social justice. *ASHE Higher Education Report Series*, 32(4). San Francisco, CA: Jossey-Bass.

Chapter Three

Enhancing EDI Initiatives through Academic and Student Affairs Partnerships

Ophelie Rowe-Allen and
Stephanie L. Burrell Storms

Some educators value a diverse campus and appreciate the exposure to various people, cultures, ideas, and worldviews. Empirical evidence demonstrates that having a diverse student and faculty population can impact higher education in a positive way (Denson and Chang, 2009). Many researchers have now focused on liberal arts education as the key to enhancing student engagement with diversity.

Liberal arts education is defined as a "...philosophy of education that empowers individuals, liberates the mind, cultivates intellectual judgment, and fosters ethical and social responsibility" (Schneider, 2008, p. 30). The stakeholders responsible for the development and execution of this philosophy are from academic and student affairs. Both serve as the institutions' frontline representatives with faculty as the embodiment of academic authority on campus (Milem, Chang, and Antonio, 2005). This chapter will describe ways in which faculty and student affairs practitioners can work together to create synergy for equity, diversity, and inclusion (EDI) initiatives.

Traditionally, student and academic affairs are seen as two separate entities relating to student learning and development in higher education. Student affairs is associated with co-curriculum, student activities, residential life, and affective or personal development, while academic affairs is linked to learning, curriculum, classrooms, and cognitive development.

After challenging the perception that student affairs and academic affairs have their own distinct and unrelated role on campus, the authors of this chapter, one from student affairs and the other from academic affairs, provide two examples illustrating how EDI can be enhanced through collaborations between the two. These strategies have been implemented at Fairfield University, a private, predominantly white, Jesuit Catholic institution. Both initiatives can be replicated at other institutions to increase students' academic progress and foster a campus culture that promotes EDI initiatives.

ACADEMIC AND STUDENT AFFAIRS PARTNERSHIPS: ESSENTIAL FOR STUDENT LEARNING

Student learning clearly takes place outside of the classroom. Professors have limited contact hours with students and assign hours of outside work for courses. Further, robust student affairs offices and programs are the norm on today's college campuses. Many faculty members who engage with first-year students will encourage them to enhance their academic and social experience by joining campus groups.

The National Student Affairs Administrators in Higher Education (NASPA) has been the leading voice for support of student success and strategic priorities for student affairs practitioners. In support of student learning and development, NASPA highlighted critical components that are important in advancing practices and competencies that are essential towards students' growth and self-exploration (Calhoun, 1996).

The following priorities guide the co-curricular programs student affairs practitioners design to help students:

> (a) develop complex cognitive skills such as reflection and critical thinking; (b) apply knowledge to practical problems encountered in one's vocation, family, or other areas of life; (c) develop an appreciation and understanding of human differences; (d) develop practical competence skills such as decision-making and conflict resolution; and (e) form an integrated sense of identity, self-esteem, confidence, integrity, aesthetic and civic responsibility. (Calhoun, 1996, p. 1)

These priorities, when combined with student learning outcomes developed through academic affairs, can prompt innovative partnerships between student affairs and academic affairs.

Partnerships between student affairs professionals and faculty are essential to the creation of successful student learning environments. When faculty and student affairs practitioners collaborate, they can have a positive effect on student learning and development. Whitt, Nesheim, Guentzel, Kellogg, McDonald, and Wells (2008) posit that academic and student affairs can bridge the gap between the academic, social, and affective elements of students' experiences.

This partnership can maximize the impact and quality of students' overall college experiences and academic outcomes, especially for students of color. As such, a case can be made for promoting intentional partnerships between student and academic affairs. Students' academic success and personal development depend not only on the quality of academic curriculum and classroom interactions but also on the work student affairs practitioners do that focuses on learning to enhance the holistic development of students in a variety of ways—including initiatives that focus on EDI.

ACADEMIC AND STUDENT AFFAIRS INITIATIVES FOR EDI

Creating a campus climate that supports EDI goes beyond racial composition and cultural vitality and more towards the curricular and co-curricular development and support and engagement of students. The work of the two entities can create cross-functional, interdepartmental linkages that combine resources and expertise to address the learning and development of students (Whitt et al., 2008). The focus on advancing the representation of traditionally underrepresented groups is a sign of progress for EDI.

Other areas are imperative to the advancement of EDI efforts, as well. These can be classified into two areas: interaction/involvement and specific programs/initiatives. Student involvement consists of engaging in intergroup dialogue, use of cultural spaces, and participation in a student organization. On the other hand, university programs and initiatives entail the structure of the core curriculum, academic support for college transition, transforming classroom spaces, on-campus living, and university policies and procedures. Supporting EDI initiatives under these two umbrellas can highlight how the university is integrating, supporting, and embracing EDI into its mission, identity, and operations.

Educational access, support, and student success, in addition to high-quality learning, are imperative to making colleges and universities distinct and inclusive. According to the Association of American Colleges and Universities (AAC&U), it is an active process that requires universities to

> uncover inequities in student success, identify effective educational practices, build practices organically for sustained institutional change, while promoting a welcoming community that engages all its diversity in the service of student and organizational learning. (2015)

The following program and undergraduate course are examples of diversity, equity, and inclusion that are departmental and university-wide efforts focusing on learning-centered diversity initiatives and building a cohesive relationship between faculty and student affairs professionals.

Academic Immersion Program

Racial/ethnic minorities and first-generation and low-income students have difficulty navigating college during their first year (Strayhorn, 2010). Fairfield University has strived to develop programs and services to provide a welcoming and accommodating environment for students. The Academic Immersion (AI) program is one such program designed to support underrepresented students.

The AI Program is a two-year program funded by the Student Diversity and Multicultural Affairs Office (SDMA), and Project Excel, a TRIO Student Support Services program funded by the US Department of Education. The first part of the program starts in the summer and continues into the first two years of the students' college journey. The program focuses on increasing the retention and persistence of culturally diverse students.

At Fairfield, underrepresented students include first-generation students, students of color, and students with disabilities. Also, all students who are Pell grant recipients are eligible for this program. The program selects up to forty students each year.

During the summer preceding their first college semester, students enroll in two college courses—one in the sciences and the other in philosophy—with coordinated co-curricular learning activities that focus on study skills, a sense of belonging (identity development), and the transition from high school to college. In addition, the program aims to enhance students' success in and commitment to particular majors, especially those in Science, Technology, Engineering, and Mathematics (STEM).

The success of this program starting in the summer is made possible from the relationships developed with faculty members to address the noticeable academic and transitional concerns. Faculty members and courses are selected based on the academic skills students need to develop and those instructors who have an interest and commitment to working with underrepresented students.

The faculty members selected and the student affairs professionals who coordinate the program discuss the challenges underrepresented students face as they transition to college. These challenges are taken into consideration as the faculty develop their course curriculum.

Some of the teaching strategies faculty employ include active learning and collaborative projects, peer teaching support for skill development, and early intervention for students struggling academically through prompt feedback from instructors. Faculty members also provide updates on academic concerns within the classroom to the SDMA and Project Excel staff members.

The co-curricular portion developed by the program coordinators in SDMA and Project Excel foster student integration into university culture and campus life. These staff members provide support services for students ranging from tutoring, study skills activities, to mentoring, coaching, counseling, and social-bonding opportunities.

The SDMA office and Project Excel work closely with counseling students in the Graduate School of Education and Allied Professions to provide coaching and one-on-one counseling in what are called "listening circles." The listening circles are group development activities that help students to build community and support their transition. Students continue to receive these services during their first two years to support their full integration academically and socially into the university.

Studies have shown that students enrolled in summer bridge programs are retained at a higher rate during their first and second years of college (Strayhorn, 2011). These early intervention experiences reduce stereotype threat (see Steele and Aronson, 1995) and help students manage the isolation and marginalization they might encounter as they navigate the collegiate experience.

The guiding principles associated with this program include structure, engagement, academic rigor, student-centered learning, high expectations, data collection, and assessment. The assessment and data collection beyond implementation focus on retention rates, academic progress/student success, and student involvement. At Fairfield, the program coordinators plan to examine the persistence and graduation rates in addition to the measures listed above.

Black Lives Matters Course

Another principle of good EDI practice for academic and student affairs partnerships involves teaching together. It is uncommon for student affairs practitioners to teach courses at a university outside of first-year experience programs. However, in 2014, students at Fairfield University held protests in support of the Black Lives Matter movement.

These protests resulted in the formation of a group called "Racial Justice is Social Justice" that comprised faculty, staff, and students to address the campus climate on race. This group became more than bystanders to the experiences of students of color. Students, faculty, and staff were interested in examining the EDI efforts at Fairfield University. Students created a set of demands, including opportunities for courses to focus on race and racism. In response to that demand, an interdisciplinary course was formed called *Black Lives Matter* (BLM) and was launched in the spring of 2016.

The BLM course was designed to provide a safe space for students to explore the "historical, geographical, cultural, social, and political ways in which race has been configured and deployed in the United States" (Garvey,

2016). Faculty from across academic disciplines and student affairs practitioners were invited to draw on their area of expertise to help students interrogate race and racism and learn about the BLM movement.

There is an instructor of record (from any discipline) that is constant throughout the semester who lectures, facilitates class discussions, and grades student work. The BLM course is three-credit hours and satisfies the US diversity graduation requirement for the core curriculum. The goals and objectives for the course (K. Sealey, personal communication, January 5, 2018) are:

- Students will understand why black lives matter.
- Students will use course materials in their responses to contemporary issues pertaining to race and racism (domestically and globally).
- Students will be able to contextualize race and racism historically, politically, and culturally.
- Students will be empowered to (1) identify and (2) disrupt acts of racism using multi-disciplinary intellectual frameworks.

A BLM working group, consisting of a small group of faculty, sends a call for proposals to faculty and staff interested in serving as guest lecturers. The working group selects approximately ten faculty and student affairs practitioners based on a summary of their proposed lesson plan.

The faculty are asked to address one of the following topics in their proposals: "race and immigration, colonialism, race and American politics, historically situating the current Black Lives Matter movement, race and healthcare, mass incarceration, race and education, stereotyping/the psychology of racism, and race and hip hop (aesthetics and the Black diasporic experience, broadly construed)" (K. Sealey, personal communication, January 5, 2018).

Once selected, the lecturers must agree to lead one seminar-style discussion (co-teaching is appreciated), attend a faculty development workshop, design an assignment to evaluate student learning based on their lesson, and mentor students as they develop their own social action projects—a requirement for the course (K. Sealey, personal communication, January 5, 2018). Through a private fund, all lecturers received a small stipend for their participation.

Both authors of this chapter were lecturers. In 2016, the author from academic affairs, an Associate Dean and Associate Professor in Multicultural Education, lectured about racial inequality and African Americans' experiences in public schools. In 2017 and 2018, the author from student affairs, an Associate Dean for Residence Life and Director of Student Diversity and Multicultural Affairs, lectured about racial bias in the media (2017) and social identity development (2018).

The student affairs practitioners that volunteered to participate each semester are staff of color. Their presence and perspective in the course were crucial due to the lack of black/African American faculty on campus. Student affairs professionals spend a great deal of time with the students outside the classroom and can offer valuable insights on topics regarding diversity and inclusion that often arise outside the classroom, particularly in the residence halls. The staff has firsthand knowledge of how students internalize and process difficult topics such as racial microaggressions.

The student affairs practitioners' unique perspectives and strategies encourage students to answer essential questions relating to diversity and inclusion. Some of the critical discussion questions led by staff members include the benefits and challenges of living in a diverse society and making connections across differences (similarities and differences that impact relationships based on identity groups).

Moreover, the staff has an opportunity to learn and understand how students internalize difficult topics and how they process the information in a classroom setting. It provides context as to how and what things are manifested as students develop their capacity to appreciate and understand differences in a shared environment.

Developing partnerships between student and academic affairs, such as the examples presented in this chapter, can show how members of the university are making a concerted effort to build a community for diversity and inclusion. In addition, the kind of pedagogy described in this chapter reveals the synergy that can be created when student and academic affairs partner to connect a wide range of diversity and inclusion issues across the university.

Moreover, it shows the commitment to identifying the resources that can enhance and shift the culture of diversity and inclusion, as well as the importance of interlocking the academic with the co-curricular life of the university.

CONCLUSION

Faculty and student affairs practitioners provide supportive learning environments for students' growth and development. Their stories offer insight into the type of work to be done for institutional change to accommodate differences in students' demographic profiles and learning. The actions of the faculty and student affairs practitioners together identify the appropriate amount of challenge and support to ensure student success without marginalizing them.

Institutions that engage in these types of initiatives recognize that different students need different kinds of support for learning and to achieve a sense of belonging. The authors believe these best practices can increase EDI within and beyond the classroom.

Yet, there is plenty of work ahead for institutions and those interested in ensuring that EDI becomes a prominent part of an institution's identity. Sustained effort is required to create extensive engagement with different partnerships across campus—especially academic and student affairs. Furthermore, there are experts within the campus community who have the experience to develop a roadmap to advance EDI by leveraging existing successful initiatives while embracing new and innovative ideas that will be beneficial to all.

REFERENCES

Association of American Colleges and Universities. (2015). Committing to equity and inclusive excellence: A campus guide for self-study and planning. Retrieved from https://www.aacu.org/sites/default/files/CommittingtoEquityInclusive Excellence.pdf.

Calhoun, J. C. (1996). The student learning imperative: Implications for student affairs. *Journal of College Student Development*, 37(2), 188–22.

Denson, N., and Chang, M. J. (2009). Racial diversity matters: The impact of diversity-related student engagement and institutional context. *American Educational Research Journal*, 46(2), 322–53.

Garvey J. (2016). *Black lives matter* [Syllabus]. Fairfield, CT: Black Studies Department, Fairfield University.

Milem, J. F., Chang, M. J., and Antonio, A. L. (2005). *Making diversity work on campus: A research-based perspective*. Washington, DC: Association American Colleges and Universities.

Schneider, C. G. (2008). Liberal education takes a new turn. *National Education Association Almanac of Higher Education*, 29–40.

Strayhorn, T. L. (2010). When race and gender collide: Social and cultural capital's influence on the academic achievement of African American and Latino males. *The Review of Higher Education*, 33(3), 307–32.

Strayhorn, T. L. (2011). Bridging the pipeline: Increasing underrepresented students' preparation for college through a summer bridge program. *American Behavioral Scientist*, 55(2), 142–59.

Steele, C. M., and Aronson, J. (1995). Stereotype threat and the intellectual test performance of African Americans. *Journal of Personality and Social Psychology*, 69(5), 797–811.

Whitt, E. J., Nesheim, B. E., Guentzel, M. J., Kellogg, A. H., McDonald, W. M., and Wells, C. A. (2008). Principles of good practice for academic and student affairs partnership programs. *Journal of College Student Development*, 49(3), 235–49.

Part II

CREATIVE APPROACHES TO RESISTANCE TO EDI GOALS

Chapter Four

Teaching about Institutional Discrimination and Personal Responsibility

Amy Eshleman, Jean Halley, and Victoria Felix

Educators who seek to challenge students to think critically about equity, diversity, and inclusion (EDI) should anticipate that students are likely to be uncomfortable with, and even resistant to, learning about the injustice that has created inequality, homogeneous institutions, and exclusion. Examples of student resistance are explored in the present chapter, including an acknowledgment that students may interpret lessons about injustice through a mental filter that seeks to absolve them of personal responsibility.

In this chapter, two approaches to effective teaching for EDI are explored; the first approach focuses on evidence of institutional discrimination before addressing personal responsibility, and the second requires a sustained focus on discrimination despite predictable initial resistance from students. These approaches increase the potential for students to become powerful upstanders who affect peers beyond the classroom.

Many students in college classrooms have passively benefited from a cultural narrative that works against recognizing inequality (Sue et al., 2007), presents diversity in a way that strips it of complexity (Halley, Eshleman, and Vijaya, 2011), and fails to promote honest consideration of what successful inclusion would mean (Halley and Eshleman, 2017). These students are likely to perceive prejudice and discrimination only regarding acts of individuals and to be unaware of institutionalized bias that affords them a privileged status (Tatum, 2017).

They might claim, "I just treat people the way I would like to be treated," and assume that they are absolved of further thinking about EDI. Because challenges to one's worldview are disconcerting (Hartwell et al., 2017), those privileged by the status quo may want to avoid seeing injustice (Ono, 2010; Tatum, 1992). Therefore, students may search for flaws in evidence of injustice that unfairly aids them—seeking a justification to reject ideas that would be unsettling (Crandall and Eshleman, 2003).

EXAMPLES OF STUDENTS' RESISTANCE TO SEEING INJUSTICE

A student benefitting from white privilege who thinks of racism as individual acts of bad people rather than a system of institutionalized injustice may resist Beverly Daniel Tatum's (2017) argument that white people[1] must choose to be actively anti-racist, as the alternative is to be racist. Given systemic injustice in the United States, to be anything but actively anti-racist, including passivity, is to be racist. Tatum defines racism as racial prejudice plus social power that comes only with whiteness.

White students who have been passive in regard to racism may seek to resist critical examination of Tatum by looking for a reason to disregard her argument—a justification for claiming that Tatum is biased and inaccurate. Given how beautifully Tatum writes her invitation to honest consideration of race, educators might imagine students' position difficult if seeking to label Tatum as problematic.

Tatum (2017) emphasizes clarity of definitions as critical for effective conversation. When communicating about racial bigotry, Tatum explains not only how she defines racism but also why she adopted a definition focusing on racism as a system of injustice. Tatum recognizes that those in conversation with her might feel strongly that the term should be defined differently. Within such interactions, Tatum notes, "I respectfully say, 'We can agree to disagree.'" When those in conversation understand how each person uses terminology, Tatum argues effective communication has a chance.

In one classroom discussion of Tatum (2017), a reliably careful reader and generally exemplary student seemed to seek a rational-sounding excuse to resist recognizing the power of white privilege. The student appeared to interpret Tatum's explanation through a lens that looked only for flaws in the argument, specifically by reading "We can agree to disagree" not as an invitation to continue the conversation despite different perspectives but rather as a flippant conclusion designed to end genuine discussion and dismiss anyone whose perspective differs.

The student expressed that she took offense at Tatum's words; the instructor realized that this was only possible by interpreting a part of one small sentence out of context. The student's tone prompted the instructor to wonder whether the student had applied a stereotype of an angry black woman while reading Tatum. Other students quickly piled on, suggesting Tatum was racist for claiming that only whites could be racist.

In another example of resistance to seeing injustice, students unprepared to acknowledge white privilege frequently look for flaws when assigned to read Peggy McIntosh's (2007) description of the phenomenon and list of ways she has been systematically privileged. One of the authors of this chapter would mentally brace herself for the onslaught of criticism when discussing McIntosh in class. Rather than reading McIntosh with an open mind, students often seemed to skip over most of McIntosh's introduction and skim the items in her list, looking for a flaw to discredit the work in its entirety.

Favorite targets of this tactic included arguing over options for finding one's flesh tone in bandages or blaming individuals who feel excluded during meetings. Such criticism tended to focus on arguing there were plenty of ways that people of color could gain equality and be included, if only they tried hard enough.

Prior to developing an understanding of privilege from an institutionalized perspective, students who benefit from privilege are more likely to feel personally attacked while reading a powerful piece revealing privilege. This prompts the use of a mental filter, focusing on evidence and absolving oneself of personal responsibility. Using a mental filter of personal absolution may also provide a framework for shifting responsibility onto others, making it especially difficult to focus on institutional factors.

Students may be motivated to disregard the evidence of institutionalized privilege for political reasons, or they may miss the institutionalized explanation because a mental filter blames others, focusing on dispositional arguments. Mental filtering of this sort applies to life beyond reading for a college course; critical examination of systems may help students to see the larger picture in other contexts rather than focusing only on trying to absolve themselves of blame.

TWO EFFECTIVE APPROACHES

The first example of misreading Tatum (2017) was surprising because the educator expected most students to approach Tatum as inviting a difficult conversation and creating an opportunity for communication to flourish. As the exam in that course approached, several weeks after the initial discussion of what Tatum meant by "agreeing to disagree," the instructor invited students' questions. The careful reader sheepishly raised her hand.

The instructor was curious because this student always seemed confident when preparing for exams. Indeed, the instructor had used this student's exams to enhance her own notes for discussions in future semesters. Rather than asking a question, the student described that her exam preparation had prompted her to read Tatum again.

The student reported that she now understood racism from Tatum's perspective and saw that Tatum's invitation to agree to disagree was an open, not insolent, gesture. Several students chimed in that they had also come around to Tatum's perspective on racism and to respect her willingness to engage in conversation with those who disagreed with her. The initial resistance had been unexpected, but this change in perspective was astounding. The instructor reflected on the change of attitude and wondered how she might try to recreate this in future classes.

The seeds of an epiphany came in the next class in which the instructor taught McIntosh (2007). As usual, the instructor braced herself for students trying to pick McIntosh apart. The instructor began the discussion by inviting students to identify items within McIntosh's list that they particularly wanted to discuss. The instructor expected students to come armed with arguments that McIntosh's mention of flesh tones of bandages discredits the piece or to blame individuals who feel excluded.

A student's hand shot passionately into the air, and the student read an item the instructor had always considered one of the most persuasive on the list. Bewildered as to why a student would pick such a strong item on which to base an argument against McIntosh, the instructor asked what aspect of that item the student wanted to discuss. The student replied that the item stood out as an excellent example of the importance of McIntosh's argument.

The discussion proceeded with students identifying items they found insightful. The instructor was delighted but wondered what had happened. Why had this group of students responded so differently to McIntosh? Could the instructor recreate this openness to learning about privilege in future courses?

Establishing Institutional Discrimination Before Exploring Individual Responsibility

Reflecting on the surprising openness to McIntosh (2007), the instructor realized that the context in which these students read McIntosh was dramatically different from previous iterations of the course. These students were exposed to McIntosh within a collection of courses in a newly comprised learning community. McIntosh was now read within the context of Andersen and Hill Collins (2007), an anthology that provides a framework focused on revealing systematic bias and injustice in a way that prompts a mental filter through which to understand privilege from a macro, rather than personal, perspective.

Therefore, students are prepared to be open to McIntosh because racism, sexism, and classism are understood as institutionalized forms of oppression rather than just behaviors that make individuals bad people. The pieces within Andersen and Hill Collins offer a foundation establishing systems of power that preclude equality.

In this context, students who unintentionally benefit from privilege may not be caught off guard or feel personally attacked. This provides an opportunity for students to focus on evidence facilitating understanding of institutionalized discrimination rather than feeling compelled to search for evidence that they are not personally responsible, for example, for people of color feeling excluded during meetings.

Sustained Focus Overcomes Initial Resistance

These examples suggest two paths to meaningful teaching for EDI; both require sustained focus (Paluck and Green, 2009). One path requires educators to weather initial resistance, trusting that repeated exposure will reach many students who will come to an openness for the material. This path is initially unpleasant both for students and educators but has the potential to produce lasting changes in attitudes (Festinger, 1957).

The other path is imminently more pleasant and consistent with Hartwell and colleagues' (2017) critical examination of how to build from awareness to knowledge, through skills, and into action. By first establishing institutionalized discrimination, more students will be prepared to think critically about privilege. This path is likely to be at least as effective as the path of initial resistance (Burgess, van Ryn, Dovidio, and Saha, 2007) and may have the added benefit of modeling a less defensive communication strategy for engaging in dialogues beyond the classroom.

Educators who establish institutional discrimination as a way of improving later discussions of personal responsibility may empower students to recognize approaches that decrease defensiveness and facilitate openness when engaged in these types of conversations, therefore increasing students' motivation to become transformative upstanders.

INSPIRING STUDENT UPSTANDERS

College campuses have the potential to provide opportunities for students to engage in dialogues that can truly overcome the bias that blocks EDI efforts (Steele, 1999). Activities in classrooms, assignments, and experiential learning (Hartwell et al., 2017) can prepare students to have a powerful impact on peers who have unexamined privilege, as well as those who have developed justifications to protect their privileged status (Nelson, Dunn, and Paradies, 2011).

The case of Derek Black is certainly not typical, but his college experience is illustrative (Tippett, 2018). When Black enrolled in a liberal arts college in 2010, he was active in the white nationalist movement, hosting a radio show on his father's Stormfront website (Bondarenko, 2017). He had launched his own white nationalist webpage at age 10, designed to attract children (Saslow, 2016).

Black was not just an atypical college student but was also unusual among white nationalists. Saslow describes, "So many others in white nationalism had come to their conclusions out of anger and fear, but Derek tended to like most people he met, regardless of race. Instead, he sought out logic and science to confirm his worldview."

Many of Black's fellow students became aware of his white nationalism when a peer revealed it on an online forum for all students at New College. In response, a student suggested, "We have a chance to be real activists and actually affect one of the leaders of white supremacy in America" (Saslow, 2016).

Matthew Stevenson answered this call and invited Black to his weekly Shabbat dinner, a truly diverse gathering of students regardless of faith background and including multiple races. Rather than confronting Black, Stevenson chose to include him in conversations that provided opportunities for peers to become upstanders who talked honestly and openly about racism, anti-Semitism, and bias against Muslims.

Black's peers listened to his justifications and dismantled them one by one by sharing scientific evidence of institutionalized discrimination, explaining race as a social construct, and revealing privilege. These conversations—prompted within the college experience—slowly chipped away at Black's justifications until he was ready to disavow white nationalism.

Although few students have Black's connections to white nationalism, many are exposed to media messages that discredit working toward EDI. Examples abound, such as rejecting discussions of economic inequality by scapegoating individuals who receive public assistance (Rose, 2000) and using a pejorative label—"snowflake"—to disregard social justice work of young people (Alyeksyeyeva, 2017).

When National Football League players sought to raise awareness about police violence and racism by kneeling during the playing of the national anthem, the protests were often reframed as dishonoring the flag (Hohman, 2017). Rather than engaging in a conversation about racism and institutionalized violence, attempts were made by some media sources and pundits to claim that the athletes were disrespecting veterans (Olson, 2017).

Both instructors in the classroom and successful student upstanders may be most effective if they anticipate attempts to discredit social justice work—recognizing efforts to change or end discussion to prevent an honest examination of systemic power.

CONCLUSION

As Tatum (2017) notes, blaming the problems of injustice on those most harmed by the injustice allows those who are privileged to avoid feelings of responsibility or guilt. Tatum identifies that guilt is often unproductive, prompting denial rather than critical examination. She clarifies that no individual is responsible for injustice that occurred before that person had the power to affect change. However, everyone is responsible for addressing injustice that currently exists.

Teaching for equality, diversity, and inclusion should seek to inspire students to accept responsibility for understanding injustice and acting within one's spheres of influence. Educators should be prepared for some students to resist critical examination. Sustained effort in the classroom increases the opportunity to reach students, who then have the potential to become changemakers with their peers.

NOTE

1. The intentional decision not to capitalize white as a racial category distinguishes the present critical examination of white privilege from how white supremacists may refer to the racial category.

REFERENCES

Alyeksyeyeva, I. O. (2017). Defining snowflake in British post-Brexit and US post-election public discourse. *Science and Education a New Dimension: Philology, 143*, 7–10.

Andersen, M. L., and Hill Collins, P. (Eds.). (2007). *Race, class, & gender: An anthology* (6th ed). Belmont, CA: Wadsworth.

Bondarenko, V. (2017, August 23). A man who was raised to be a die-hard white nationalist explains what it took for him to rethink his beliefs. *Business Insider.*

Burgess, D., van Ryn, M., Dovidio, J., and Saha, S. (2007). Reducing racial bias among health care providers: Lessons from social-cognitive psychology. *Journal of General Internal Medicine, 22*, 882–87.

Crandall, C. S., and Eshleman, A. (2003). A justification-suppression model of the expression and experience of prejudice. *Psychological Bulletin*, 129, 414–46.

Festinger, L. (1957). *A theory of cognitive dissonance.* Stanford, CA: Stanford University Press.

Halley, J., and Eshleman, A. (2017). *Seeing straight: An introduction to gender and sexual privilege.* Lanham, MD: Rowman & Littlefield.

Halley, J., Eshleman, A., and Vijaya, R. M. (2011). *Seeing white: An introduction to race and white privilege.* Lanham, MD: Rowman & Littlefield.

Hartwell, E. E., Cole, K., Donovan, S. K., Greene, R. L., Burrell Storms, S. L., and Williams, T. (2017). Breaking down silos: Teaching for equity, diversity, and inclusion across disciplines. *Humboldt Journal of Social Relations*, 39, 143–62.

Hohman, H. (2017, October 4). The reframing of the Kaepernick debate. *The Stanford Daily.*

McIntosh, P. (2007). White privilege: Unpacking the invisible knapsack. In M. L. Andersen and P. Hill Collins (Eds.), *Race, class, & gender: An anthology* (6th ed., pp. 98–102). Belmont, CA: Wadsworth.

Nelson, J. K., Dunn, K. M., and Paradies, Y. (2011). Bystander anti-racism: A review of the literature. *Analyses of Social Issues & Public Policy*, 11, 263–84.

Olson, Y. S. (2017, September 26). "Total disrespect all around": Lake County veterans respond to NFL protests. *Lake County News-Sun.*

Ono, K. A. (2010). Postracism: A theory of the "post-" as political strategy. *Journal of Communication Inquiry*, 34, 227–33.

Paluck, E. L., and Green, D. P. (2009). Prejudice reduction: What works? A review and assessment of research and practice. *Annual Review of Psychology*, 60, 339–67.

Pronin, E., Lin, D. Y., and Ross, L. (2002). The bias blind spot: Perceptions of bias in self versus others. *Personality and Social Psychology Bulletin*, 28, 369–81.

Rose, N. E. (2000). Scapegoating poor women: An analysis of welfare reform. *Journal of Economic Issues*, 34, 143–57.

Saslow, E. (2016, October 15). The white flight of Derek Black. *The Washington Post.*

Steele, C. M. (1999). Thin ice: Stereotype threat and black college students. *Atlantic Monthly*, 248, 44–54.

Sue, D. W., Capodilupo, C. M., Torino, G. C., Bucceri, J. M., Holder, A. M. B., Nadal, K. L., and Esquilin, M. (2007). Racial microaggressions in everyday life: Implications for clinical practice. *American Psychologist*, 62, 271–86.

Tatum, B. D. (1992). Talking about race, learning about racism: The application of racial identity development theory in the classroom. *Harvard Educational Review*, 62, 1–24.

Tatum, B. D. (2017). *"Why are all the Black kids sitting together in the cafeteria?" and other conversations about race.* New York: Basic Books.

Tippett, K. (Host). (2018, May 17). Interview with Derek Black and Matthew Stevenson: How friendship and quiet conversations transformed a white nationalist. *On being.*

Chapter Five

Managing Your Own Socio-Emotional Landscape

Theodora P. Williams, Stephanie L. Burrell Storms, and Sarah K. Donovan

Instructors teaching about equity, diversity, and inclusion (EDI) often confront some "messiness" in dealing with challenges in the classroom. EDI instructors need to become sensitive to their own competencies, such as self-awareness, self-regulation, motivation, empathy, social skills, relationship management, and effective communication (Goleman, 2006).

This chapter begins with a discussion of the difficulty in having open conversations about differences in the higher education classroom and some examples of when it goes wrong. It then explores three topics that may help faculty manage their own socio-emotional landscape in those moments: (1) setting the tone, (2) dealing with "impostor syndrome," and (3) managing personal triggers.

In her seminal work, *A Tale of "O,"* Kanter and Stein (1980) expound on the experiences of being different in group settings (workplace). In the Western world, people are often acculturated to see things in binary terms—red state/blue state, rich/poor, male/female, black/white, gay/straight, North/South. Binary thinking can foster discontinuity and disagreement (Burns, 2016).

The Pew Research Center, citing longitudinal data gathered since 1994, which has focused increasingly on political polarization since 2014, documented how this phenomenon is apparent in political discourse and divisive policy debate with the result of a more polarized society. Since 2014, research found that 87 percent of American adults feel there is a widening gap in political dialog (Pew Research, 2014). The college classroom is not immune.

Instructors and students alike struggle to find the right words to discuss differences in meaningful and respectful ways. For instructors, there is a range of ways in which they have experienced discomfort in the classroom through what students have said to them, what they themselves have said, or what they don't know how to say.

In one example, two white male students were so uncomfortable when their female African American professor told them that affirmative action benefits white women that they said loudly in unison, "That is a lie!" How do professors manage the complexities of race, gender, and authority in moments like these?

In a second example, a cisgender faculty member teaching gender studies mistakenly used the outdated term "hermaphrodite" instead of "intersexed" and was (respectfully) corrected by a student in front of the class. How do professors negotiate their role as "the one who knows" with the possibility that they might publicly use the wrong language?

For a third example, a cisgender faculty member doesn't know the preferred gender pronouns of a student who didn't fit into the male/female binary and felt uncomfortable assuming or just ignoring it. How do professors ask students about their identities without offending them?

For students, there are many moments when they contribute to the class in ways that are intentionally provocative or unintentionally insensitive. For example, a professor asks students to participate in a class activity where they share aspects of their personal identity. A male student shares that he immigrated legally to the United States. As he talks about his cultural identity, he shares a Donald Trump sticker and says, "Trump is my guy." How do professors negotiate the introduction of polarizing politics in a discussion about personal identity?

In another example, a student who is genuinely trying to participate in a positive way in a discussion about race clearly has not internalized the appropriate language and uses the term "colored people" instead of "people of color." How do professors correct inaccurate and hurtful language in front of the class without shaming students?

A well-known movie scene helps capture these dynamics: the cantina scene that invariably shows up in each Star Wars series movie. The cantina is typically a nightclub on some neutral planet where various species can socialize and interact. There are obvious visual and social differences. Sometimes they manage their socio-emotional landscapes and connect to each other, and other times they do not.

The cantina is a microcosm for the diverse classroom. Some days it is a happy cantina where differences are celebrated and respected. Other days, it is adversarial, and difference is suspect or devalued. It is in the latter instances when professors need to be leaders who know how to manage their own socio-emotional landscapes and model it for students.

SETTING THE TONE (BECAUSE THESE CONVERSATIONS ARE *GOING* TO HAPPEN)

Triggering statements, microaggressions, awkward discussions, and unconscious or implicit bias. All these descriptors are real and may manifest themselves in the classroom. Often, instructors' efforts to address them are based on unexamined assumptions or constraints on their individual professional development and responsibility.

Although many institutions have established promising EDI initiatives with a focus on curricular changes, hiring practices, and professional development, it is a challenge for some faculty who are engaged in discipline-specific teaching and research to recognize and address issues of identity, power, and privilege. Referring to these issues with the umbrella term "inclusive teaching" can be problematic.

A proven strategy in such circumstances that sets the right tone for the class is to craft diversity and inclusion language on the syllabus. Such statements and/or classroom discussion agreements are a more standard fixture in the social sciences, business, and the humanities, and they are not always the norm in science, technology, engineering, and mathematics (STEM) classes. However, creating such a document requires a partnership between faculty and students. Though an incremental step, this type of document can be integrated into any course.

Eliciting discussion and feedback from the students can result in a useful dialog where differences of opinion can be voiced and respected. Simply asking the students what they would like included in a diversity and inclusion syllabus statement sets the tone and encourages strategic use of the course syllabus. Requesting that students prioritize their concerns signals the value an instructor places on student input. This prioritization could be accomplished by using a Likert scale to rank student concerns, which will also alert the instructor to commonalities and differences among the class members.

Another technique for obtaining useful feedback from students is having each student complete a data-gathering, getting-to-know-you form at the beginning of the course. In addition to pertinent information such as a can-be-reached phone number, alternate email address, and the best time of day to reach the student, the request also could include, "How should I address you in class (A nickname? Use of middle name instead of a first name?)," "Which pronouns do you prefer for yourself?," "What would make this course easier for you?," and "What would improve the quality of course materials for you?" (Linden, n.d.).

Such feedback could be requested in a welcoming statement, on the course site in your learning management system, or in-person at the beginning of the term, making it clear that the instructor values diversity of perspectives and experiences and respects individual identities. These tools could be shared with other faculty members through the faculty assembly or senate, in a newsletter, or through the institution's Teaching and Learning Center website, where information about teaching practices is broadly disseminated. Such strategies reinforce the instructor's desire to empathize, motivate, and communicate effectively.

IMPOSTOR SYNDROME

Feelings of self-doubt and the fear of being exposed as an imposter can be just below the surface for educators who teach social justice education. "Imposter syndrome" has been defined as an "internal experience of intellectual phoniness" predominantly found among high-achieving women (Clance and Imes, 1978). It is important to name this issue so social justice educators can recognize these negative thoughts, interrupt them, and engage in difficult conversations without fear of being outed as a fraud.

Feeling not smart enough or lacking credibility might be particularly powerful when professors with majority privileged identities teach about the oppression of marginalized groups. Men teaching about sexism, whites teaching about racism, and cisgender women and men teaching about transgender oppression are all examples of teaching with majority privileged identities that can potentially elicit imposter syndrome.

At the same time, these educators may feel confident, aware, and knowledgeable about the ways in which oppression affects subordinated groups, especially if they identify with those groups personally and have lived experiences as evidence.

For example, a professor who identifies as differently abled teaching about ableism and a Jewish instructor teaching about anti-Semitism may, in each case, demonstrate deep awareness of the injustices associated with that group. Instructors who identify as gay or lesbian may feel more comfortable discussing how they have been harmed by heterosexism but not how they benefit from classism.

However, to teach about the many faces of oppression and how their intersectionality is exhibited, professors must be courageous and educate students about topics they feel "less qualified" to teach. This involves realizing that all professors who engage in difficult conversations will make mistakes eventually. When that happens, professors need to be prepared to acknowledge the mistake and apologize. Reframing the mistake as a learning opportunity can reduce discomfort.

Educators who feel like imposters can address these feelings by first examining their own social identities and acknowledging the status of each as either dominant or non-dominant. This exercise in critical self-knowledge is a lifelong journey. The goal is not to reach some imaginary level of critical consciousness but to be open to nuanced ways in which statuses provide advantages and disadvantages.

A simple exercise instructors can use to begin this process is completing a Social Identity Wheel[1] ("Social Identity Wheel," 2017) themselves, labeling each of their identities with a "D" (dominant group) or "S" (subordinated group), and then using this information to research how they benefit from or are a target for discrimination.

They can then take what they learn to set the stage on the first day of class. Instructors can introduce themselves using only their social identities (i.e., black, upper-middle-class, Christian, cisgender, etc.). This may help educators feel less like imposters when they are upfront about their own identities, admit they had to learn about people who are differently positioned, and acknowledge with students that they, the professors, are also on a journey.

It is normal for instructors to stumble when teaching about social justice issues that they know less about due to privilege, and they should ask for help. One of the goals of the socialization process is to keep advantages and disadvantages based on social identity hidden so that the cycle of oppression stays in place.

Therefore, it is imperative that instructors acknowledge when they need help so that they can draw on the skills and experiences of those whose voices are often muted in higher education but who are highly knowledgeable as social justice educators. These educators may be in the same department, in the same school or college, in student affairs or other parts of the college or university, or in the local community. They could be brought in as guest lecturers and/or could co-teach with the instructor or with students.

Institutions must examine how their policies and practices might contribute to perpetuating the imposter syndrome. Scholars contend that faculty can be made to feel like imposters due to the lack of diversity in their fields and rewarding those whose teaching and research is considered mainstream (e.g., implicit bias during the hiring process and tenure and promotion decisions) (Dancy and Jean-Marie, 2014; Revuluri, 2018).

Therefore, it is important that administrators and faculty share instructional strategies so that they can create structures to support the work of those engaging in social justice education (or who want to engage). As an example, a Center for Teaching and Learning can create a workshop series or a learning community where educators have critical conversations about teaching for EDI.

DEALING WITH PERSONAL TRIGGERS

Regardless of how much instructors have engaged with topics related to EDI on an academic level, they are still human beings who have feelings and reactions. This may be especially relevant for instructors who defy the stereotype of who an instructor is in higher education.

Rather than trying to imagine every situation that could trigger an instructor to feel in a way that doesn't seem "professorial," this section draws on one general instructor/student dynamic that is ripe for triggers. The section then explores three concrete ways in which the dynamic might play out, four reasons why it triggers, and four possible responses. This exercise helps instructors short circuit a visceral reaction and do what they do best—teach and model respect.

Who hasn't found themselves in the situation of "instructor as defense attorney"? In this situation, students self-appoint as "prosecutors" and maintain that their worldview is innocent of issue x, y, or z until the instructor can convince said students, beyond a reasonable doubt, that their worldview is "guilty." Here are three concrete examples of how this might play out.

One, a white student raises his hand during a class on affirmative action and states that his white friend didn't get into Harvard while an allegedly less-qualified person of color did because of reverse racism against white people. The student is challenging the faculty member to defend the claim that racism against people of color in admissions or hiring is real.

Two, a student raises her hand during a class about gender inequality and tells the instructor that she has never experienced sexism and that women are completely equal to men in the twenty-first century. The student is challenging the instructor to defend the claim that gender inequality is real.

Three, a student raises his hand during a class about issues affecting the LGBTQ community and says that his religion says that anything that deviates from heterosexuality is morally wrong. The student is challenging the instructor to defend the claim that issues affecting the LGBTQ community are real moral issues that aren't eclipsed by the student's religious morality.

When students ask instructors to play the role of a defense attorney, there are at least four reasons it can make instructors feel frustration, annoyance, self-doubt, and/or fatigue. One, it puts the instructor and the student in an adversarial relationship. Two, it makes instructors feel like they have to engage in the exercise of confronting an alternate reality often not supported with facts. Three, it sets up instructors for failure when complex issues are presented in divisive or unsophisticated binary terms that will set up sides where someone "wins" and someone "loses." Four, it could derail the entire class discussion.

Instructors are human and can be prone to knee-jerk reactions, but four strategies help instructors decline the role of the defense attorney as they manage their own socio-emotional landscape.

One, instructors can pause and ask other students for their perspectives.

Two, regardless of the tone of the question, instructors can choose to be generous and ask the students for clarification. Students are generally in our classrooms because they have much to learn. Students don't always say what they mean or mean what they say.

Three, instructors can mirror for students what the question sounded like, in a gentle manner, by weeding out language or tone that would shame students; students may genuinely not know how insensitive what they have said sounded. Instructors can then help the student frame the question so that it is more productive.

Finally, if students are genuinely on the attack, instructors can gently pull them back to the established ground rules. While students can express their opinion—it is their First Amendment Right—the classroom must have ground rules that state that class members must have respect for each other and that ask students not to participate in any speech or behavior that violates student codes of conduct regarding language and harassment.

Instructors can also ask students to ground what they are saying in the course readings. Sometimes this leads to a realization that students are misinterpreting what they read. Sometimes it leads students to realize that they cannot just say what comes to mind, but they must also have evidence that supports their views.

CONCLUSION

In the end, students are going to push buttons, and professors will be tempted to react. Having strategies in place will minimize faculty reactions that may impede instruction and learning. It is essential that social justice educators shore up their own self-awareness (and admission of their own vulnerabilities), create a classroom environment that is open and effective, and feel competent and confident while doing so.

These strategies are provided to combat student resistance by setting the tone, recognizing and countering imposter syndrome, and managing triggers. These strategies also help instructors to recognize and discuss issues around identity, power, and privilege. As educators, we know that only through identifying and breaching borders, along with recognizing and interrogating our own assumptions, can we successfully educate students to become transformative in their own spheres of influence in order to become change agents for social justice.

NOTE

1. The Social Identity Wheel worksheet is an activity that encourages students to identify and reflect on the various ways they identify socially, how those identities become visible or more keenly felt at different times, and how those identities impact the ways others perceive or treat them.

REFERENCES

Burns, K. (2016). *Ken Burns Jefferson Lecture*. National Endowment for the Humanities. Washington, DC, May 9, 2016.

Clance, P. R., and Imes, S. A. (1978). The imposter phenomenon in high achieving women: Dynamics and therapeutic intervention. *Psychotherapy: Theory, Research & Practice*, 15(3), 241–47.

Dancy, T. E., and Jean-Marie, G. (2014). Faculty of color in higher education: Exploring the intersections of identity, impostorship, and internalized racism. *Mentoring & Tutoring: Partnership in Learning*, 22(4), 354–72.

Goleman, D. (2006). *Social Intelligence*. New York: Random House.

Kanter, R. M., and Stein, B. A. (1980). *A tale of "O": On being different in an organization*. New York: Harper & Rowe.

Linden, M. (n.d.). Put it in the syllabus. *Tomorrow's Professor*, Retrieved from https://tomprof.stanford.edu/posting/1625.Pew Research. (2014). *Political Polarization in the American Public*. Retrieved from www.pewresearch.org/fact-tank/2018/07/26.

Revuluri, S. (2018, October 4). How to overcome imposter syndrome. *The Chronicle of Higher Education*. Retrieved from https://www.chronicle.com/article/How-to-Overcome-Impostor/244700.

Social Identity Wheel. (2017). Retrieved from https://sites.lsa.umich.edu/inclusive-teaching/wp-content/uploads/sites/355/2018/12/Social-Identity-Wheel-3-2.pdf.

Chapter Six

Fostering Inclusivity through Social Justice Education: An Interdisciplinary Approach

Paul Carron and Charles McDaniel

Teaching at a private, predominantly white religious institution in Texas poses unique challenges for equity, diversity, and inclusivity (EDI). Many of the students at the institution discussed in this chapter come from a broadly evangelical Christian background, a tradition with many contemporary voices disparaging social justice as too "liberal." Furthermore, attending this private, tuition-driven institution means high tuition and, while financial aid is comparable with peer institutions, many of the students come from relative economic privilege.

Given these factors, it is necessary to first introduce students at this institution to the contemporary realities of inequality and oppression and, thus, the *need* for EDI. This chapter proposes a conceptual framework and pedagogical suggestions for teaching basic concepts of social justice in an interdisciplinary social sciences course. The course integrates four different approaches to justice: theoretical, social scientific, narratological, and experiential. The chapter offers an overview of each approach. The discussion of the experiential dimension of the course references practical strategies for making social justice and inequality real for our students.

Such pedagogical strategies provide students with an understanding of the realities of social inequality and its roots and foster a better understanding of the social forces and structures that perpetuate inequality. Furthermore, this approach can plant the intellectual and empathic seeds to challenge in-group bias, thereby stimulating fruitful interaction with diverse others. Finally, this rich, interdisciplinary encounter with social inequality and justice can prepare students to work for just social structures that will lead to a more inclusive world.

"What is justice?" provides the conceptual framework for a two-semester, team-taught social science course in an interdisciplinary core program.

Justice is an inherently multi-disciplinary concept, ideal for an interdisciplinary social science course that begins with foundational readings from the Western philosophical canon.

Significant works in contemporary psychology, sociology, economic theory, and political philosophy follow. These readings include an extended sociological study of the black middle class in contemporary America and the disadvantages that African Americans face due to the history of racism in America, along with the structural forces that continue to perpetuate racial inequality.

These sociohistorical studies reinforce philosophical claims that a just cultural and political order is essential for individual flourishing. Bringing together theoretical and social scientific perspectives allows students to see the reality of social forces. We contend that all four approaches need to work together to help privileged students unfamiliar with difference to truly empathize with others. While it is ideal to have two semesters to do this work, we can envision faculty incorporating different parts of our longer course sequence into an effective one-semester course.

THEORETICAL APPROACHES

Plato's *Republic* and Aristotle's *Nicomachean Ethics* introduce the question "What is Justice?" For Socrates and Aristotle, justice is both a personal virtue (a quality of the *psuché* or "soul") and a necessary aspect of a good, well-ordered society. Socrates concludes in Book IV of Plato's *Republic* that justice emerges from a well-ordered soul and a well-ordered society. Internally harmonized individuals possess justice because they are guided by wisdom and are not overcome by the desire for honor or profit (Plato, 1991, MN443d).

Just individuals have well-balanced souls where every psychological faculty does its part; societal justice is similarly achieved when everyone minds their own business and fulfills their societal role (Plato, 1991, MN433b). Therefore, justice is a "negative" social virtue in the *Republic* in the sense that it involves individuals not infringing upon the roles and duties of other citizens.

Aristotle writes in the *Nicomachean Ethics* that justice is a *particular personal virtue* that "deals with honor, material goods, security, or whatever single term we can find to express all these collectively"; moreover, it is the *whole of virtue*, since "...the best man is not the one who practices virtue toward himself but who practices it towards others...." (Plato, 1991, MN1130b1-5, and MN1130a5-10). Justice is the only *social* cardinal virtue; it turns the individual outwards towards the needs of the other and prevents the craving for more than one's share of societal goods.

Just individuals are disposed to take their fair share and no more, ensuring that others receive *their* due. Personal justice promotes a just society where everyone receives their proper share or what is owed them. These readings introduce students to the ethical, psychological, sociological, economic, and political dimensions of justice.

SOCIAL SCIENTIFIC APPROACHES

Beginning with philosophical conceptions of justice shows students the deep roots of the idea of a just society in Western intellectual culture. Furthermore, beginning with these ancient sources is persuasive for those students who are inclined to take *tradition* as an important source of authority.

Crucially, the philosophical understanding of societal justice and its relationship to personal flourishing facilitates the turn to contemporary scientific explorations of justice. We begin discussing these perspectives in the first, more-theoretical semester by integrating several psychological theories.

For example, while reading Plato, students learn about the contemporary notion of cultural emotion regulation (CER). CER stipulates that culture largely determines how its members view the world. Cultural complexes "constitute a person's reality, because they focus attention, they guide perception, they lend meaning, and they imbue emotional value" (Mesquite and Albert, 2007, p. 288). CER proponents emphasize the psychological and moral influence of cultural complexes, indicating that cultural views causally influence the self's psychological tendencies.

For example, whereas a member of an individualistic culture generally seeks personal fulfillment and happiness, a member of a collectivistic culture often feels a strong sense of social obligation and interdependence (Kitayama, Markus, Matsumoto, and Norasakkunkit, 1997; Levine, Norenzayan, and Philbrick, 2001). Those complexes provide parameters for how people experience and regulate their emotions. Since cultural complexes largely constitute the individual and lend meaning and value to one's life, personal fulfillment requires just social structures.

Focusing on the birth of the modern social sciences provides a sociological perspective on justice in the second-semester course. Karl Marx introduces the class to notions of social inequality and the role of societal structures in constituting the individual. Marx's concept of historical materialism is the idea that "the nature of individuals thus depends on the material conditions determining their production" (Marx and Engels, 2010, p. 33). Individuals are constituted by their material, economic conditions, and workers without property suffer alienation because of their dire conditions.

Emile Durkheim, Max Weber, and W. E. B. Du Bois provide early empirical support for social structures. For instance, Durkheim's study of suicide as a sociological phenomenon evidences that "individual pathologies are rooted in *social* conditions" (Edles and Appelrouth, 2010, p. 119). This finding gives rise to Durkheim's notion of social facts—social or cultural realities that shape the individual's values and behaviors (Durkheim, 2010, pp. 112–13).

Du Bois engages the question of social inequality in his study of African Americans in Philadelphia and observes, for example, that blacks receive low wages for undesirable work (mostly household and service sector labor) and are charged more money for lower quality housing than their white counterparts (Du Bois, 2010, pp. 340–43). Du Bois highlights social facts that make it more difficult for African Americans to flourish.

Contemporary research reflected in Michelle Alexander's *The New Jim Crow* and Ta-Nehisi Coates's "The Case for Reparations" drives home these early findings. Alexander and Coates trace the history of laws and customs in America that severely limited the rights of African Americans, showing the contemporary reverberations of these unjust social structures.

Coates, for instance, traces the history of discrimination in the housing industry, highlighting practices such as redlining, where the Federal Housing Administration (FHA) labeled neighborhoods "according to their perceived stability….Neighborhoods where black people lived were rated 'D' and were usually considered ineligible for FHA backing. They were colored in red" (Coates, 2014).

Coates draws on historical data to argue that housing discrimination isn't merely an historical fact but continues today, as seen in the profound difference between the average wealth of middle-class black and white households with the same income (Shapiro and Oliver, 1995; Sharkey and Pew Charitable Trusts, 2009). Historic racist social structures continue to reinforce inequality.

Alexander opens her book with a similar method of argumentation, showing how racial hierarchy and the subordination of African Americans is deeply embedded in America's cultural practices and laws, beginning with chattel slavery, morphing into Jim Crow laws, and manifesting today in the mass incarceration of African Americans. She notes that between 1960 and 1990, the US incarceration rate quadrupled (Alexander, 2012, p. 7).

Since African Americans are incarcerated at more than five times the rate of whites, she labels mass incarceration as the New Jim Crow. These data-driven historical studies highlight how social structures constrain individual agency and reinforce those theoretical positions on social justice that students encounter early on in our Social World sequence.

NARRATOLOGICAL APPROACHES

Theoretical and scientific approaches are compelling to some students, but many remain unconvinced. After all, socially inculcated moral intuitions are not easily altered (Haidt and Graham, 2007). Furthermore, some researchers have argued that "most undergraduates are in fact not ideologically pliable. By the time they reach college, most students have developed a political point of view" (Maranto and Woessner, 2017).

As noted, many of our students come from conservative cultural and religious backgrounds and relative economic privilege. They often assume that the individual can overcome social forces through hard work; thus, it is not social structures that perpetuate inequality but individual agency.

These last two pedagogical strategies—narrative and encounter—are intended to overcome such skepticism. Examples of narratological approaches are an extended ethnographical study of a black middle-class neighborhood in Chicago and several short films.

Mary Pattillo's *Black Picket Fences*, set in the 1990s, describes life for African Americans living in "Groveland," a pseudonymous black middle-class neighborhood in Chicago's Southside. Pattillo presents a wealth of sociological data and stories of individuals told in their own words.

Although unique in certain respects, Groveland resembles similar middle-class neighborhoods that developed in large part due to redlining. These neighborhoods are just outside the inner city—they were suburbs when originally developed—and comprised of mostly African Americans, many of whom have owned their homes for generations.

Neighborhoods like Groveland are different from otherwise similar predominantly white neighborhoods: they border the inner city, where crime, drugs, and homelessness are usually most prevalent, exposing residents to illicit behavior that suburbanites typically do not encounter.

Furthermore, the local public schools often have poor graduation rates, high teacher turnover, and failing test scores. Our students learn of the struggles that teenagers living in Groveland face and how hard it is for them to succeed, given all the cards stacked against success.

Films such as Morgan Spurlock's *30 Days: Minimum Wage* and the biography of Cesar Chavez—*Fight in the Fields*—offer students more opportunities to enter into someone else's story and *imagine* what it would be like to struggle against overwhelming social forces.

Spurlock's attempt to live on minimum wage for 30 days enables some students to envision how difficult life is for those on the margins. Studies in empathy show that people identify stronger and have stronger positive feelings with people that they take to be part of their in-group (Xiaojing et al., 2009).

These narratological accounts are a crucial aspect of a social justice education because imagination is critical to empathy, and empathy is essential to prompt students to care for people in different life situations.

EXPERIENTIAL APPROACHES

The narratological approach is a pedagogical response designed to engender understanding and empathy in our students. However, the narrative approach still leaves an experiential gap between the student and the other. Closing this gap is aided by students *encountering* others face to face, forcing a reevaluation of assumptions that promote alienation rather than identification. When encountering the other in concrete circumstances, the student must grapple with another human being in their particularity and struggle, making it more difficult to disassociate the other and dismiss their experience.

The course provides several opportunities for students to encounter the other. When reading Weber on class, status, and party, and learning about Cesar Chavez's efforts to organize immigrant farmworkers in *Fight in the Fields*, a panel of Latino Americans speaks to the class and answers questions about their experiences living and working in Texas.

Similarly, when reading Coates, Du Bois, and Pattillo, an African American panel consisting primarily of local leaders meets with our students. Students prepare for the panel sessions by developing questions for panelists whose biographies are provided. However, most student questions are generated in the dynamic interaction between the panelists and the students, providing a rare encounter with members of the community.

These first-hand encounters make it difficult for students to discount the experiences of those who live and work in the same space as they do, providing a powerful and hopefully transformational moment.

Another opportunity for an encounter is our version of experiential learning, where the students visit one of several philanthropic organizations that aid the working poor in our community. These "field-site" visits occasion both a mini sociological investigation and engagement with both service providers and clients.

For example, students who visit the Waco Family Health Center (WFHC) are confronted with the reality of poverty and the lack of access to adequate health care for those on the margins. They learn how the combination of poverty and lack of health care leads to negative consequences, such as a disproportionate number of premature births (Henderson, 1994).

From the Texas Hunger Initiative, students learn about the state's high rate of childhood food insecurity, which is unfathomable considering that Texas has the second-largest gross state product in America.

The class session following the site visits provides the opportunity for debriefing and discussion; the reactions of students are palpable. Most students simply have no idea how many people are suffering in their own community and how difficult it is to escape the cycle of poverty.

Part of the assignment is to connect what they witnessed during their field-site visit to our theorists, providing students the opportunity to relate the ethics and social theory they engage in the classroom with contemporary life and practice.

The combination of field-site visits and the subsequent classroom reflections on those experiences is rated consistently as one of the most meaningful and pedagogically important course elements by students in their course evaluations at the end of the semester.

CONCLUSION

While our course was developed as a two-course sequence, by condensing the readings, the use of speaker panels and field-site visits might be incorporated into a one-course format, especially if students are more disciplinarily homogeneous.

For example, within a business-management course, a panel of business leaders on labor practices could be complemented by student site visits to local companies where employees from human resources and other departments are observed and interviewed.

The intent of our course design is to help students understand the importance of breaking down barriers that prevent inclusivity. However, the inherently insular nature of our campus, as well as the university's largely homogeneous student population, require that forms of "barrier deconstruction" are designed into the curriculum.

Combining theoretical explorations of social justice with empirical verification, narratological approaches, and first-hand encounters with community inspires the kind of empathy necessary for the development of a personal ethic, an important first step in social justice education.

REFERENCES

Alexander, M. (2012). *The new Jim Crow: Mass incarceration in the age of color-blindness*. New York: New Press.

Aristotle. (1999). *Nicomachean Ethics* (M. Ostwald, Trans.). Upper Saddle River, NJ: Prentice-Hall, Inc.

Coates, T.-N. (2014, June). The case for reparations. *The Atlantic*. Retrieved from https://www.theatlantic.com/magazine/archive/2014/06/the-case-for-reparations/361631/.

Du Bois, W. E. B. (2010). The Philadelphia Negro (1899). In L. Desfor Edles and S. Appelrouth (Eds.), *Sociological theory in the classical era: Text and readings* (pp. 340–45). Thousand Oaks, CA: Pine Forge Press.

Durkheim, E. (2010). The rules of sociological method. In L. Desfor Edles and S. Appelrouth (Eds.), *Sociological theory in the classical era: Text and readings* (pp. 112–19). Thousand Oaks, CA: Pine Forge Press.

Edles, L. D., and Appelrouth, S. (2010). Introduction to suicide: A study in Sociology. In L. Desfor Edles and S. Appelrouth (Eds.), *Sociological theory in the classical era: Text and readings* (119–122). Thousand Oaks, CA: Pine Forge Press.

Haidt, J., and Graham, J. (2007). When morality opposes justice: Conservatives have moral intuitions that liberals may not recognize. *Social Justice Research*, 20(1), 98–116.

Henderson, J. W. (1994). The cost effectiveness of prenatal care. *Health Care Financing Review*, 15(4), 21–32.

Kitayama, S., Markus, H. R., Matsumoto, H., and Norasakkunkit, V. (1997). Individual and collective processes in the construction of the self: Self-enhancement in the United States and self-criticism in Japan. *Journal of Personality and Social Psychology*, 72(6), 1245–67.

Levine, R. V., Norenzayan, A., and Philbrick, K. (2001). Cross-cultural differences in helping strangers. *Journal of Cross-Cultural Psychology*, 32(5), 543–60.

Maranto, R., and Woessner, M. (2017, July 31). Why conservative fears of campus indoctrination are overblown. *The Chronicle of Higher Education*. Retrieved from https://www.chronicle.com/article/Why-Conservative-Fears-of/240804.

Marx, K. (2010). Economic and philosophical manuscripts of 1844. In L. Desfor Edles and S. Appelrouth (Eds.), *Sociological theory in the classical era*: *Text and readings* (pp. 42–50). Thousand Oaks, CA: Pine Forge Press.

Marx, K., and Engels, F. (2010). The German ideology (1845–1846). In L. Desfor Edles and S. Appelrouth (Eds.), *Sociological theory in the classical era*: *Text and readings* (pp. 33–40). Thousand Oaks, CA: Pine Forge Press.

Mesquite, B., and Albert, D. (2007). The cultural regulation of emotions. In J. J. Gros (Ed.), *Handbook of emotion regulation*. New York: Guilford Press.

Plato. (1991). *The Republic of Plato: Second edition* (Allan Bloom, Trans.). New York: Basic Books.

Shapiro, T. M., and Oliver, M. L. (1995). *Black wealth/white wealth: A new perspective on racial inequality*. New York: Routledge.

Sharkey, P., and Pew Charitable Trusts. (2009). *Neighborhoods and the black-white mobility gap*. Washington, DC: Economic Mobility Project.

Spurlock, M., Virgil Films (Firm), and FX (Television network). (2010). *30 days: The complete series*. New York: Virgil Films & Entertainment.

Xu, Xiaojing, Zuo, Xiangyu, Wang, Xiaoying, and Han, Shihui. (2009). Do you feel my pain? Racial group membership modulates empathic neural responses. *The Journal of Neuroscience*, 29(26), 8525–29.

Part III

INSTITUTION-WIDE INITIATIVES

Chapter Seven

CIRCLE: A Research Center for EDI Initiatives

Angela Fink, Erin D. Solomon, and Regina F. Frey

This chapter describes the mission and methods of a university-supported education research center focused on higher education, examining how the center's equity, diversity, and inclusion (EDI) initiatives rely on and create new connections among faculty, administrators, and staff. The chapter begins with a history of the research center, the Center for Integrative Research on Cognition, Learning, and Education (CIRCLE) at Washington University in St. Louis (WashU).

The next section outlines three guiding principles that make CIRCLE's EDI initiatives collaborative and expansive in reach. The remainder of the chapter explores three initiatives led by CIRCLE and its collaborators, aimed at improving EDI within the university's science, technology, engineering, and mathematics (STEM) departments. The chapter concludes with recommendations for generalizing the principles and practices observed in this case study to other institutions with different missions, campus climates, and resources.

A HISTORY OF CIRCLE

WashU has been working on improving teaching and learning and increasing EDI for many years. In 2008, a small group of faculty interested in EDI and evidence-based teaching more generally, who also had an institutional educational grant from the Howard Hughes Medical Institute (HHMI), began meeting weekly in a community of practice (Wenger, McDermott, and Snyder, 2002).

The community used a laboratory-group model, where members discussed their education-research projects with the purpose of sharing expertise and stimulating collaborations. Developing from these discussions, CIRCLE was founded in 2011 with initial support from the Office of the Provost and is co-directed by two faculty members from different disciplines (Chemistry and Psychology). It has grown to include research scientists, graduate students, and internal and external faculty collaborators while maintaining both internal and external funding to support research and implement programs.

CIRCLE's mission is to provide a bridge between WashU's faculty and researchers in the psychological sciences, learning sciences, and discipline-based education research to facilitate collaborative projects that improve student learning, attitudes, and engagement. The center's EDI work was initially spurred by faculty concerns about the classroom experiences of student groups who are underrepresented at our institution (e.g., Pell-eligible students) or in STEM fields (e.g., women).

The composition of WashU's student body is approximately 53 percent female, 50 percent white and not multiracial, 30 percent Asian, and 20 percent underrepresented minority, with Pell-eligible students increasing from 6 percent to 14 percent in the past five years. This focus on underrepresented groups strengthened as CIRCLE's research revealed that faculty concerns about underrepresented students were worth investigating further, even after cognitive-based learning interventions were implemented to support the success of all students.

GUIDING PRINCIPLES FOR CIRCLE'S EDI INITIATIVES

Following recent scholarship on diversity and institutional change in higher education, three research-based principles of practice guide the design and implementation of CIRCLE's initiatives. First, CIRCLE uses data to demonstrate how EDI objectives are relevant in any academic context, even when they are not central to course content. Research suggests that successful EDI initiatives require a willingness to reflect on how pedagogical practices, course procedures, and organizational structures influence the outcomes for diverse students (Kezar Glenn, Lester, and Nakamoto, 2008).

CIRCLE, therefore, models and engages the campus community in evidence-based reflection. During community meetings (e.g., faculty meetings and professional-development events), CIRCLE shares data that illustrate how students' identities can affect their academic achievement and persistence and how EDI initiatives can improve the outcomes of all students, especially those from marginalized groups. The center then engages the meeting participants in small-group discussions, where they interpret data relative to their own courses and reflect on changes they might make with CIRCLE's support.

Second, CIRCLE establishes long-term relationships between EDI experts and faculty, administrators, and student-support staff, so the campus community receives ongoing support while they learn about, pilot, and refine EDI techniques over time. Engaging the community in continuous EDI-oriented reflection is critical for institutional change because it can transform peoples' thinking and spur them to greater action (Bensimon, 2004).

Maintaining relationships between practitioners and EDI experts helps CIRCLE convey that increasing EDI is a collaborative and ongoing process that engages all community members, rather than an outcome unto itself (Milem, Chang, and Antonio, 2005).

Third, CIRCLE seeks buy-in from university leadership (e.g., department chairs and deans), who are positioned to endorse and incentivize EDI initiatives. Such top-down support is an essential "strategic lever" for enacting a successful, sustainable EDI initiative (Williams and Clowney, 2007; Kezar, Glenn, Lester, and Nakamoto, 2008). When initiatives are decentralized and engage many stakeholders with different perspectives, leadership can validate and illuminate how EDI relates to the institution's overall mission.

Also, high-level administrators have the discretion to reward participation in EDI initiatives (e.g., course releases or special recognition). Such rewards may increase community participation at the outset of EDI initiatives and increase the likelihood that such initiatives will become institutionalized (Allen-Ramdial and Campbell, 2014; Williams and Clowney, 2007).

OVERVIEW OF CIRCLE'S EDI INITIATIVES

Three CIRCLE-led initiatives are described in this section, which vary concerning their scope, funding sources, and strategies for achieving EDI objectives. The first two initiatives supported EDI indirectly by promoting faculty usage of active and evidence-based teaching strategies, which foster better and more equitable student outcomes in STEM (e.g., Haak, HilleRis-Lambers, Pitre, and Freeman, 2011; Lorenzo, Crouch, and Mazur, 2006). The third initiative represents the culmination of the prior two; it was sought and secured specifically to build the university's capacity for EDI exploration and programming.

Nonetheless, all three initiatives share the principles of evidence-based reflection, long-term relationships, and top-down support to encourage broader EDI engagement among faculty, administrators, and staff.

Initiative 1: AAU Active-Learning Initiative

CIRCLE's first EDI initiative was funded by a grant from the Association of American Universities (AAU) as part of its Undergraduate STEM Education Initiative, which arose from national reports recommending the adoption of active and evidence-based teaching in undergraduate STEM education (Brewer and Smith, 2011; Olson and Riordan, 2012). As the AAU Active-Learning Initiative at WashU took shape from fall 2013 to spring 2017, the center's guiding principles helped generate lasting change.

First, the Active-Learning Initiative promoted a multi-strategy approach to incorporating active and evidence-based teaching into the undergraduate STEM curriculum, thereby engaging a wider range of faculty. Multiple points of entry to curricular change were encouraged, inviting faculty and departments with different experience and comfort levels to implement strategies that suited their course objectives and teaching personas. For example, when comparing two large introductory courses at WashU, the instructors varied in their prior experience with evidence-based curriculum design.

The instructors of one course, having no prior experience, made moderate curricular changes during the Initiative, adopting the well-established pedagogy of clicker review questions (Caldwell, 2007). In contrast, the instructors of the other course, with more experience implementing evidence-based strategies, made more extensive changes, adopting a Peer-Instruction variation (Mazur, 1997) and testing a growth-mindset intervention (Fink et al., 2018). Thus, CIRCLE expanded participation in its Active-Learning Initiative by making it relevant and accessible to all experience levels.

Second, the Active-Learning Initiative created new professional-development faculty events and programs, so interested individuals could learn about the latest STEM education research and receive support while implementing new teaching techniques. For instance, the Summer STEM Faculty Institute on Teaching (STEM FIT) was established, where WashU faculty could participate in three days of interactive workshops and working-group sessions to design the implementation and evaluation of evidence-based teaching practices.

After the inaugural STEM FIT in 2014, the event expanded to include faculty from other institutions in the region. In 2017, previous STEM FIT participants attended a one-day STEM FIT Symposium, where they shared their experiences testing and assessing curricular innovations. The success of the STEM FIT series and Symposium, which will alternate years going forward, demonstrates the value of establishing long-term relationships among those committed to evidence-based, inclusive teaching.

By the end of the grant period, CIRCLE's Active-Learning Initiative had a demonstrable impact: fourteen academic departments/programs, seventy-one-course sections, and fifty faculty members had adopted new evidence-based teaching and learning strategies. The positive impact of this initiative persuaded the Office of the Provost to provide institutional funding for CIRCLE's next project, the Transformational Initiative for Education in STEM.

This transition from external to internal funding illustrates the importance of buy-in from campus leadership, whose commendations and practical support are needed to sustain EDI initiatives.

Initiative 2: Transformational Initiative for Education in STEM

CIRCLE's second EDI initiative, from fall 2016 to spring 2020, had objectives similar to the Active-Learning Initiative; however, those goals were achieved using a modified approach. Specifically, the Transformational Initiative aimed to (1) improve diverse students' learning, performance, and engagement through evidence-based teaching practices; (2) and evaluate the impact of those evidence-based strategies, especially for underrepresented groups, thereby enabling data-driven reflection (Kezar et al., 2008).

Additionally, the initiative aimed to (3) create infrastructure that supports departments in continuous program improvement, promoting the idea of EDI as a process, not an outcome (Milem, Chang, and Antonio, 2005); and (4) continue collaborations with faculty who began implementing and evaluating evidence-based strategies under the Active-Learning Initiative, while also developing new collaborations.

To achieve these goals, the Transformational Initiative drew inspiration from Carl Wieman's Science Education Initiative (Wieman, 2017). Rather than recruiting individual faculty, Wieman's approach engages whole academic departments to facilitate broader cultural change. Following Wieman, the Transformational Initiative operationalized this approach by embedding experts—Education Specialists—within participating departments.

The Education Specialists became discipline-based education researchers, who possess expert knowledge of their disciplines and are specially trained in pedagogy. They performed dual roles, participating fully in CIRCLE laboratory meetings and research projects, while also providing resources and support to the departments where they were embedded. The Education Specialists devoted much of their time to working with faculty who were engaging in EDI exploration, redesigning their courses using evidence-based practices and presenting their work at learning community events.

After the Transformational Initiative began, CIRCLE continued strategizing ways to connect diverse campus partners in a shared effort to increase the success of all undergraduates, especially in STEM. The center capitalized on the relationships built during the Active-Learning and Transformational Initiatives to build an institution-wide project team for its third and most expansive EDI initiative to date.

In collaboration with STEM faculty and department chairs, the Dean of the College of Arts and Sciences, and the Division of Student Affairs, CIRCLE received a five-year Howard Hughes Medical Institute (HHMI) Inclusive Excellence grant (2017–2022), which is funding a campus-wide project to improve the educational experience of first- and second-year students interested in STEM. The project, described in the next section, exemplifies how successful EDI initiatives simultaneously rely on and create new connections among faculty, administrators, and student-support staff.

Initiative 3: HHMI Inclusive Excellence Project

The HHMI's Inclusive Excellence grants are named after the latest model of diversity in higher education—Inclusive Excellence—which conceives of diversity as an essential ingredient for academic and institutional success, whose value must relentlessly be affirmed through integrated, strategic EDI plans and programs (Williams, Berger, and McClendon, 2005; Williams and Clowney, 2007). To enact this philosophy, CIRCLE's Inclusive Excellence project focuses on increasing the EDI awareness, knowledge, skills, and action orientation of stakeholders who interact with first- and second-year STEM students.

This group includes faculty in lower-level STEM courses, undergraduate peer leaders, and four-year-advising and student-affairs staff. The project purposely aims to improve undergraduate STEM education by focusing on faculty and student-support staff as intervention targets rather than directly targeting students.

Key representatives from each stakeholder category, some of whom worked with CIRCLE since its foundation, made a two-year commitment to participate in professional-development training with a working group of colleagues. These working groups are learning about the latest research on EDI issues, reflecting on how those issues manifest in their day-to-day interactions with students, and generating concrete strategies for addressing them. The groups then implement, evaluate, and refine at least one strategy with their students, with ongoing support from CIRCLE and the Inclusive Excellence project team.

Thus, the Inclusive Excellence project is engaging faculty, administrators, and staff in a shared process of EDI exploration while also tailoring that exploration to the needs of their specific roles so all community members are prepared to achieve a consistent narrative of success in STEM for all students.

For example, the Inclusive Excellence faculty program was formed by having STEM department chairs nominate instructors of lower-level courses to participate. Each year, faculty participants are expected to attend three workshops and to collaborate with CIRCLE and the Inclusive Excellence project team on curricular changes. After completing the two-year training program, faculty participants are invited to join a community of practice (Wenger, McDermott, and Snyder, 2002) called the CIRCLE Teaching Academy.

This community regularly gathers for events and discussions focused on inclusive, evidence-based teaching in STEM. For instance, CIRCLE commenced the Teaching Academy Speaker Series in Spring 2019. The series invites one nationally known speaker to WashU each semester who has expertise in the psychological sciences, learning sciences, and discipline-based education research.

In addition to a keynote presentation, the speaker meets with small groups of interested STEM faculty within their departments to explore how the instructors might implement the presented strategies to achieve EDI objectives in their own classrooms.

Going forward, new Teaching Academy members will be drawn from various CIRCLE-led faculty-development programs. The focus of Teaching Academy events will evolve as the community advances in their EDI exploration, evidence-based teaching techniques, and evaluation skills. CIRCLE and the Inclusive Excellence project team intend for this community of practice to become institutionalized, thereby maintaining long-term relationships.

CONCLUSIONS

CIRCLE, an education-research center at WashU, is well-situated to connect faculty, administrators, and staff in EDI initiatives. The center has secured a combination of internal and external funding, which enables it to develop large-scale, multi-faceted projects. It has strong ties to the STEM departments with which it collaborates, via co-directors who are STEM faculty and carry teaching loads, embedded experts (Education Specialists), and buy-in from department chairs.

Because CIRCLE's staff possess both research and pedagogical expertise, they not only can recommend curricular innovations but also engage the community in reflecting on why and how those innovations support the success of all students.

Despite CIRCLE's unique circumstances, its three guiding principles are grounded in the literature on diversity and organizational change in higher education and could help any individual, department, or institution establish collaborative EDI initiatives. What follows is a synthesis of the principles and practices observed in this case study, which may help readers generalize the ideas to their own environments:

- Collaboratively use data to inform practice. Provide opportunities for faculty, administrators, and student-support staff to interpret and reflect on disaggregated student data, ideally by establishing an EDI-oriented community of practice that holds regular meetings. By exploring the data themselves, community members gain a deeper understanding of how students' identities can affect their achievement and well-being. Situating the iterative process of EDI exploration, intervention, and evaluation in a community creates a data-driven feedback loop that enables members to become more effective practitioners.
- Foster flexible, long-term relationships. Present multiple approaches to achieving EDI objectives, and allow individual stakeholders to select the strategy, implementation, and timeline that suits them best. Such flexibility conveys that there is no singular, "correct" method for increasing EDI. Instead, it allows participants to gradually increase their use of evidence-based strategies for student success, according to their scheduling demands, comfort level, and other factors. Long-term structures and relationships should be established among practitioners, EDI experts, and education specialists.
- Obtain support from key administrators. Determine the scope of an EDI initiative and identify administrators who are influential in that sphere. If the initiative spans multiple departments, then department chairs may serve as key "strategic levers." If it occurs within a single department/office, then administrators of different programs (e.g., directors of undergraduate or graduate studies) may be the target. Regardless of a project's scope, buy-in from key administrators can help demonstrate the value and importance of the EDI initiative.

REFERENCES

Allen-Ramdial, S.-A., and Campbell, A. G. (2014). Reimagining the pipeline: Advancing STEM diversity, persistence, and success. *BioScience*, 64(7), 612–18.

Bensimon, E. M. (2004). The diversity scorecard: A learning approach to institutional change. *Change: The Magazine of Higher Learning*, 36, 44–52.

Brewer, C. A., and Smith, D. (2011). Vision and change in undergraduate biology education: A call to action. *American Association for the Advancement of Science, Washington D.C.*

Caldwell, J. E. (2007). Clickers in the large classroom: Current research and best-practice tips. *CBE-Life Sciences Education*, 6(1), 9–20.

Fink, A., Cahill, M. J., McDaniel, M. A., Hoffman, A., and Frey, R. F. (2018). Improving general chemistry performance through a growth mindset intervention: Selective effects on underrepresented minorities. *Chemistry Education Research and Practice*, 19, 783–806.

Haak, D. C., HilleRisLambers, J., Pitre, E., and Freeman, S. (2011). Increased structure and active learning reduce the achievement gap in introductory biology. *Science*, 332(6034), 1213–16.

Kezar, A., Glenn, W. J., Lester, J., and Nakamoto, J. (2008). Examining organizational contextual features that affect implementation of equity initiatives. *The Journal of Higher Education*, 79(2), 125–59.

Lorenzo, M., Crouch, C. H., and Mazur, E. (2006). Reducing the gender gap in the physics classroom. *American Journal of Physics*, 74(2), 118–22.

Mazur, E. (1997, March). Peer instruction: Getting students to think in class. In *AIP Conference Proceedings*, Vol. 399, No. 1, pp. 981–88.

Milem, J. F., Chang, M. J., and Antonio, A. L. (2005). *Making diversity work on campus: A research-based perspective.* Washington, DC: Association of American Colleges and Universities.

Olson, S., and Riordan, D. R. (2012). Engage to excel: Producing one million additional college graduates with degrees in science, technology, engineering, and mathematics. Report to the President. *Executive Office of the President.*

Wenger, E., McDermott, R. A., and Snyder, W. (2002). *Cultivating communities of practice: A guide to managing knowledge.* Harvard Business Press.

Wieman, C. (2017). *Improving how universities teach science: Lessons from the Science Education Initiative.* Cambridge, MA: Harvard University Press.

Williams, D. A., Berger, J. B., and McClendon, S. A. (2005). *Toward a model of inclusive excellence and change in postsecondary institutions.* Washington, DC: Association of American Colleges and Universities.

Williams, D. A., and Clowney, C. (2007). Strategic planning for diversity and organizational change: A primer for higher-education leadership. *Effective Practices for Academic Leaders*, 2(3), 1–16.

Chapter Eight

Fellows Program: Training the Next Generation of EDI Researchers

Jacqueline Rodriquez and Natoya Haskins

In an age of heightened discrimination and polarizing rhetoric, institutions of higher education have a moral and functional imperative to make clear the values and principles they uphold. Many students and their families want to know how the university creates and promotes an inclusive environment for students from diverse racial, ethnic, socioeconomic, religious, and linguistic backgrounds. The university cannot subsist without acknowledging and responding to national calls for deep reflection coupled with purposeful action to create safe learning spaces for all students.

This chapter begins by briefly introducing the creation of the Social Justice and Diversity Graduate Research Fellows program (Fellows Program) at The College of William & Mary. It then explains how to replicate a Fellows Program by outlining the program, arguing for the need for the program by highlighting the lack of mentorship and the marginalization of equity, diversity, and inclusion (EDI) research, and developing both a course of action and scaling the action through an iterative design and reflection process.

CREATION OF THE FELLOWS PROGRAM

Reflecting on policies and practices that have perpetuated discriminatory attitudes is a requirement to becoming a "learning organization" (Watkins and Marsick, 1993; Yang, Watkins, and Marsick, 2004), which is what the authors contend should be a central component to an evolving system of higher education in the United States. The College of William & Mary responded to these imperatives by encouraging faculty and students to become "citizen scholars" and supporting the establishment of a Fellows Program.

Annually, at William & Mary, located in historically conservative Virginia, graduate students interested in pursuing research in the fields of social justice, diversity, equity, and inclusion are selected from various disciplinary fields across the campus to become Research Fellows in the Fellows Program. The primary objective of the Fellows Program is to provide access and opportunity to develop, design, and execute research in the areas of EDI.

A secondary objective is to provide mentorship to burgeoning social justice scholars. To facilitate their access and opportunity to these research areas, faculty used a Mellon Foundation Grant awarded to William & Mary to develop a course on civic leadership for the Research Fellows entitled "Social Justice."

The course can be taught by two or more faculty members from unique disciplines and covers social justice theoretical frameworks, ethical and legal issues, systemic barriers for citizens and for researchers, and culturally responsive leadership. To promote the secondary objective, Research Fellows engage in monthly professional-development activities with leaders in the fields of critical race theory, social justice, cultural responsiveness, and equity education.

OUTLINING THE PROGRAM

The Fellows Program facilitates networking and interdisciplinary collaborations, fosters an interdisciplinary understanding of diversity and social justice, supports social justice and diversity research by providing a platform for feedback, creates a space where new research projects can be discussed and promoted, and serves as a venue to garner mentoring in conducting this type of research.

Fellows are expected to enroll in one course, "Social Justice," which meets weekly and bridges both semesters. Within the course, Research Fellows identify topics of related interest with their peers and work in research groups to develop research agendas that focus on one or multiple areas for the year: diversity, equity, social justice, and advocacy. The Research Fellows are also introduced to university and national scholars (e.g., law, psychology, education, history, etc.) who are engaged in social justice and diversity research utilizing online and traditional panel formats.

Recruitment for the Fellows Program begins in the spring semester with a focus on students who are completing their first year in any graduate school discipline across the university. While incoming graduate students are often interested in joining the Fellows Program, the intensity of balancing coursework, research, and service at the graduate level is often unparalleled for many students.

The Fellows Program is a commitment of, among other things, time and cognition. Matriculated graduate students make decisions about additional responsibilities concerning other obligations with more insight and rationale. In addition, most second-year students have had an opportunity to identify their research interests and the types of research they are interested in conducting.

While the Fellows Program is a one-year commitment open to second-year graduate and doctoral students at the university, the associated course, "Social Justice," is also open to upper-level undergraduate students interested in social justice research.

With these two populations in mind, the co-directors, each from different disciplines, sought a veteran social justice researcher and faculty member with an established record to work with undergraduate students to co-develop the university course on social justice research. Current instructors represent counselor education, special education, and psychology and teach students from the undergraduate level to the doctoral level.

The course teaches content and skills to address issues of social justice, diversity, and equity in schools and within the larger community by requiring students to (1) engage in community building by participating in an annual academic course; (2) review literature in a given field in order to select research questions for their research groups; (3) collaboratively develop a literature review; (4) identify, analyze, and select an appropriate research methodology; (5) develop a timeline for data collection; (6) analyze data using qualitative and quantitative methods; and (7) submit a proposal to present the analysis and implications of the data collected.

Undergraduate students interested in the course are required to have a basic knowledge of research and have engaged in research projects within group settings. This expectation is not difficult to meet for most students as the university prides itself on the number of undergraduates who complete research during their university career. Targeting these specific populations—upper-level undergraduates with research experience, graduate and doctoral students interested in researching social justice—provides a gateway for professors to actively advise and mentor students who have foundations in research and interest in the topics.

Identifying funding and support is paramount to launching a cross-campus endeavor of this nature. While financial support from a singular entity is ideal for accounting and regulatory purposes, piece-meal funding is often necessary until proof of concept has been demonstrated. The credibility of the Fellows Program was established through several iterations of positive outcomes as measured by publication acceptance, presentations at professional conferences, and professional development on the topic of study as measured by student surveys.

THE NEED FOR GRADUATE LEVEL
RESEARCH TO STUDY EDI

Developing a Fellows Program was a response to the significant need for mentorship in the research areas of EDI and the need to help students understand the narrative that legitimizes its research methods. Mentorship has been touted as the most advantageous method to support students, especially students of color, and academics engaged in diversity-related research.

Most students conducting diversity- and equity-based research are left out of the mentoring process (Bova, 2000; Dixon-Reeves, 2003; Patton, 2009). However, scholars agree that mentoring serves to enhance the persistence and retention of female and male students (Brown, 2009; Butler et al., 2013; Patton, 2009). Specifically, graduate students' persistence and retention is based, in part, on the encouragement they receive from faculty mentors (Cuyjet, 2006; Johnson-Bailey, 2004).

While students of color are more apt to conduct research connected to their life narratives related to diversity and social issues, current researchers indicate that diversity and social justice research topics are becoming more mainstream, with students from various cultural backgrounds engaged in the EDI scholarly community (Gwyther and Possamai-Inesedy, 2009). Although the community is becoming more diverse, these scholars continue to be viewed as under-mentored and marginalized as researchers. Epistemic exclusion is felt by many scholars who choose to study EDI, and the Fellows Program helps to address this.

Epistemic exclusion refers to the devaluation of research topics and methodologies (e.g., qualitative research) that are designed to illuminate, examine, or critique the experiences of marginalized populations (Dauka, 2006; Dotson, 2012). At various universities, epistemic exclusion can serve to limit or eliminate the production of knowledge that furthers EDI scholarship.

In this regard, graduate students are advised to not conduct EDI research and are instead guided toward more mainstream research topics that might increase their job prospects and legitimacy in their field of study. Consequently, the Fellows Program provides students with the research experience and content expertise to counter this narrative ensuring they become leading scholars in the areas of EDI research.

For one example, the Fellows Program helps students to understand and combat the devaluation of a main source of its data—qualitative research. Qualitative methods (e.g., case study, ground theory, Participatory Action Research, ethnography, Consensual Qualitative Research, phenomenology, etc.) are often more ideal for students studying EDI because they allow researchers to focus in on populations that can be invisible in quantitative methods due to small sample sizes.

Addressing critics of qualitative research requires that the Fellows Program help students to become well versed in selecting and applying the appropriate research design while ensuring the validity and reliability of the study outcomes. This is useful for all faculty and students interested in EDI research.

In the Fellows Program, students from different disciplines are grouped together, and they tend to overlap regarding topic and experience. Students are encouraged to illuminate and explore the hidden or overlooked experiences of various populations and phenomenon. The interdisciplinary structure is critical to helping the Research Fellows understand how to work with various disciplines to develop and execute a shared goal.

Examples of projects include exploring cross-cultural mentoring motivations, examining the experiences of queer students at historically black colleges and universities (HBCUs), and investigating the experiences of international students at a predominantly white university.

In this regard, students were simultaneously taught effective research methodologies and encouraged to investigate the effect of mentorship on students' research experiences. For these projects, Fellows were encouraged to use a transcendental phenomenological approach (Moustakas, 1994), where they focused on attempting to understand the essence of best practices white faculty use to effectively mentor students of color (Creswell and Poth, 2018).

In addition, Fellows from different disciplines also conducted a qualitative case study on the experiences and perspectives of undergraduate international students at a predominately white institution. The purpose of this study was to describe and uncover undergraduate international students' experiences of the campus climate as well as access and use of campus community resources.

Finally, to better understand the specific needs and experiences of LGBTQ college students, the Fellows used Queer Theory to deconstruct sociocultural norms and institutions of power that determine how orthodox and deviant notions of gender and sexuality are constructed and maintained.

SCALING UP AND FUTURE PURSUITS

Much like any successful startup, being thoughtful and strategic sets the stage for optimization. In the case of setting up a Fellows Program, interested faculty must identify how they will adapt to the time commitment, dialogue and collaborate with external potential stakeholders, mentor new scholars, and seek change in the face of long-standing university norms and institutional bureaucracy. The following three starting points provide direction for interested faculty: engaging academic stakeholders, partnering with the office of diversity and inclusion, and using the Fellows Program as a recruitment tool.

Engaging Academic Stakeholders

The Fellows Program at William & Mary is championed by academic stakeholders who stream-lined administrative processes out of their desire to support these initiatives. The instructors will now collaborate with academic committees and departmental faculty within Arts & Sciences, Education, Business, and Law to include specific professional organization standards that align to the course topic within each of those disciplines. Including these standards helps students within those disciplines to receive course credit as well as programmatic credit, that is, to take the course as a part of their major, minor, or graduate-degree program.

Partnering with Relevant Offices

Offices of Diversity and Inclusion across the country are seeking opportunities to enhance their social justice and diversity footprint across campus. Partnering with these offices around an initiative such as a Fellows Program would allow these offices to engage not only with faculty that have similar values and beliefs but also the students.

Developing a relationship with diversity officers and inviting them to collaborate on Fellows Program programming is how the directors of the Fellows Program initiated a partnership. They were able to communicate how the program goals are consistent with their offices' goals and objectives. For example, because the Research Fellows are encouraged to share their research through various avenues during their program year, the Offices of Diversity and Inclusion can provide additional platforms for content to be shared with other offices and school leaders on campus.

In addition, partnering will allow the Research Fellows to engage in other social justice and diversity-focused opportunities and expand the scope of the program. Furthermore, the Diversity office has access and opportunities to apply for certain types of funding from which the Research Fellows' directors can benefit. Lastly, it is imperative that a program such as this is developed with other stakeholders on campus to ensure that all disciplines are embraced, various communities on campus understand how students' research experiences can be enhanced, and university goals are met.

Fellows Program as Recruitment

In addition to promoting collaboration among offices on campus, the Fellows Program has become a tool for recruitment. As the Fellows Program becomes more well-known and gains traction regarding recruitment across the campus community, the co-directors have observed faculty and staff introducing potential students to "an opportunity to research topics of social justice and diversity" during their graduate careers at the university. Contrary to what may appear self-serving for the faculty, the intention is to increase the footprint of social justice research being conducted on campus and to recruit students with this interest.

CONCLUSION

Finally, in keeping with the objectives to (1) increase EDI on the campus and in the community through access and opportunity to conduct social justice research and (2) to provide mentorship and guidance to burgeoning social justice researchers, the co-directors have established several ways to promote and grow the Fellows Program, the Research Fellows, and their research.

The first is a robust web presence introducing potential Research Fellows as well as potential mentors to the program. The second is to create media briefs that can be used by campus publications, university news, and external media sites. Included in the briefs are the quantitative and qualitative data collected over the course of the Fellow Program demonstrating the benefit to the students and the community.

A third way is to establish sustainable funding through institutional support or a combination of institutional, donor, grant-funded, and alumni support. Working alongside the university advancement department and the alumni department is a valuable first step in securing sustainable funding. Securing an academic component to the program, for course credit or possibly for service learning and research credit, affords latitude in how the program is marketed to potential funding outlets. It also demonstrates, through academic outcomes, the legitimacy of the program.

REFERENCES

Bova, B. (2000). Mentoring revisited: The black woman's experience. *Mentoring & Tutoring*, 8(1), 5–16.

Brown, N. L. (2009). Fusing critical race theory with practice to improve mentorship. *International Forum of Teaching and Studies*, 5, 18–21.

Butler, S. K., Evans, M. P., Brooks, M., Williams, C. R., and Bailey, D. F. (2013). Mentoring African American men during their postsecondary and graduate school experiences: Implications for the counseling profession. *Journal of Counseling and Development*, 91, 419–27. DOI: 10.1002/j. 1556-6676.2013.00113.x.

Creswell, J. W., and Poth, C. N. (2018). *Qualitative Inquiry and Research Design Choosing among Five Approaches.* (4th ed.). Thousand Oaks, CA: Sage Publications.

Cuyjet, M. J. (2006). *African American men in college*. San Francisco: Jossey-Bass.

Daukas, N. (2006). Epistemic trust and social location. *Episteme*, 3, 109–24. http://dx.doi.org/10.3366/epi.2006.3.1-2.109.

Dixon-Reeves, R. (2003). Mentoring as a precursor to incorporation: An assessment of the mentoring experience of recently minted Ph.D.s. *Journal of Black Studies*, 34(1),12–27.

Dotson, K. (2012). A cautionary tale: On limiting epistemic oppression. *Frontier: A Journal of Women Studies*, 33(1), 24–47.

Gwyther, G., and Possamai-Inesedy, A. (2009). Special issue: New methods in social justice research for the 21st century. *International Journal of Social Research Methodology*, 12, 97–98.

Johnson-Bailey, J. (2004). Hitting the proverbial wall: Participation and retention issues for outcomes. *Journal of Higher Education*, 78(2), 125–61.

Moustakas, C. E. (1994). *Phenomenological research methods.* Thousand Oaks, CA: Sage Publications.

Patton, L. D. (2009). My sister's keeper: A qualitative examination of mentoring experiences among African American women in graduate and professional schools. *Journal of Higher Education*, 80, 510–37.

Watkins, K. E., and Marsick, V. J. (1993). *Sculpting the learning organization: Lessons in the art and science of systemic change.* San Francisco: Jossey-Bass.

Yang, B., Watkins, K. E., and Marsick, V. J. (2004). The construct of the learning organization: dimensions, measurement, and validation. *Human Resource and Development Quarterly*, 15(1), 31–55.

Chapter Nine

Challenging Ableism through Community-Campus Partnerships

Cynthia Kerber Gowan and Nuala Boyle

Ableism or the marginalization and discrimination of people with disabilities is pervasive in our culture. People with disabilities face massive inequities around issues of health, economics, and education. Individuals with intellectual or developmental disabilities (I/DD) are at an increased risk of poverty because they lack both job readiness skills and job placement opportunities.

With LifePrep@Naz program as a model, this chapter will explore how a campus-based community partnership addresses this disparity, while also expanding the definition of diversity on a college campus to include ability. The topics include: disability as a social construct, the college campus as a place for inclusion, LifePrep's framework for inclusion, and measuring impact.

DISABILITY AS A SOCIAL CONSTRUCT

For many, disability is recognized as a socially constructed form of difference, similar to the ways other forms of difference are socially constructed, including race, class, and gender (Davis, 1997; Skrtic, 1995). Some researchers have investigated the use of disability as a form of exclusion, with roots in implicit bias, systemic racism, and an oversimplified understanding of culture (Artiles, Kozleski, Trent, Osher, and Ortiz, 2010; Gutierrez and Rogoff, 2003). Today's schools grapple with issues such as the overrepresentation of minorities in special education, particularly in segregated settings.

With the label of "disabled" comes the societal response of exclusion, particularly in schools, where, systemically, the idea of "normal" is perpetuated (Baglieri, Bejoian, Broderick, Connor, and Valle, 2011). This continues on through life as adults with disabilities face some of the highest rates of unemployment, suggesting that ensuring equitable access requires more than providing additional educational opportunities for persons with disabilities.

If the systemic barriers and hierarchy of status between the "abled" and the "disabled" are to be challenged or dismantled, one must begin by challenging those places where this is socially constructed. Expanding inclusive practice and providing additional access to post-secondary education for those with I/DD can begin to break down the disparities of social systems for persons with disabilities.

While institutions of higher education (IHE) may not discriminate on the basis of disability, they may still establish standards for admission. These standards create a space where individuals with I/DD are not included because the established minimum academic standards are out of reach.

While high academic standards are important to maintaining one's reputation as an IHE, the role of IHEs in perpetuating systemic cultural bias is important to examine. Inclusion, when executed successfully, can create opportunities for all students to reconceptualize difference and become advocates for social justice (Ballard, 1999; Sapon-Shevin, 2003). By creating inclusive educational spaces that purposefully challenge students to reconceptualize how they view disability, IHEs can become a place for social change that extends beyond the traditional college experience.

THE COLLEGE CAMPUS AS PLACE FOR INCLUSION

Nazareth College is dedicated to inclusion and supports experiences that actively engage students in purposeful practices and processes that both value and respect difference. The LifePrep program provides individuals with I/DD, aged eighteen and older, a college experience with the objective that graduates become self-determined and competitively employed.

LifePrep is a reciprocal partnership between Nazareth College and two community partners: Victor Central School District and The Arc of Monroe County. LifePrep students participate in both tailored and inclusive vocational trainings, internships, and life-skills development opportunities. All partners are dedicated to co-educating the LifePrep students as part of the larger college community and provide full-time support for the on-campus program.

LifePrep's goal of addressing the marginalization of persons with I/DD is met by providing opportunities for all students to experience college together. LifePrep students are afforded access to every program and resource available to their Nazareth student peers. They are fully integrated into campus social opportunities and academic life. The inclusion of students with I/DD provides opportunities for the college community to critically reflect on how disability is a social construction, understand the importance of access to college campuses, and participate in high-impact community-engaged learning.

Community-based learning, including academic service learning, not only strengthens the outcomes, success, and retention of college students but also acts as a vehicle for deconstructing identified systems of power and inequality (Bringle and Hatcher, 1995; Kuh, 2008; Mitchell, 2007).

Partnerships with community members and groups provide the IHE with the opportunity to engage and collaborate meaningfully with additional diverse voices and to build capacity for coordinated community impact. They also provide students with opportunities to apply their learning in complex, authentic settings and opportunities to reflect on their own role within the larger social system (Kuh, 2008).

In turn, the IHE can provide community partners with access to resources, both physical and intellectual, which can strengthen the mission and work of the community-based organization. These mutually beneficial experiences can be created both inside and outside of credit-bearing coursework. Varying levels of interaction, a focus on reciprocity, and critical reflection are the foundation for a successful community-based learning experience.

LIFEPREP FRAMEWORK FOR INCLUSION

Changing perceptions is paramount to increasing opportunities for people with I/DD; LifePrep improves the outcomes of its students by changing the perception of Nazareth's student body towards people with disabilities. Several components make up the LifePrep program and contribute to the overall goals of expanding the definition of diversity and challenging inequities. These components include LifePrep staffing and shared responsibilities; co-curricular and curricular integration; a mentor program; and purposeful campus engagement.

The LifePrep program is truly collaborative, sharing staffing and program responsibilities among all three partners. Staff from both community agencies work on campus in the program full-time, and the college has faculty and staff time dedicated specifically to the program. While each of the three agencies has individual responsibilities, they collectively provide educational programming for both the LifePrep and Nazareth College students.

The LifePrep program leverages the resources of all three partners who work in tandem to co-administer the program. This is made possible through consistent and structured communication, collaborative goal setting, and shared record keeping. The combined resources from the college, adult agency, and school district provide depth to the program and positive outcomes for all stakeholders.

With the LifePrep students on campus, several departments realized an opportunity to engage their students in important curricular experiences, including service-learning, internships, and research. These relationships are reciprocal and designed to meet the learning goals of both the Nazareth and LifePrep students.

Students in professional programs in the Communication Sciences and Disorders, Physical Therapy, Art Therapy, Occupational Therapy, Education, and Social Work departments engage in learning experiences that provide opportunities to meet graduation and licensure requirements while simultaneously meeting the needs of the LifePrep students in developing skills in areas such as communication, self-advocacy, stress management, and healthy living.

These relationships have grown and evolved over time. For example, in the last few semesters, Nazareth students have engaged more directly in working collaboratively with the on-campus staff from the community partners. These experiences impact the larger community by providing scaffolded learning experiences that lead to vital skill development students take into their fields as professionals.

LifePrep students audit a Nazareth course each semester. These courses are from every department across campus and at various academic levels. Professors opt into the program, making an active decision to host a student in their course. The LifePrep students choose courses that interest them and their learning goals are individualized.

Their participation is also designed to help them learn important social, time-management, and communication skills vital to success in the workplace. In addition to the outcomes for LifePrep students, Nazareth students are also learning in these courses, participating in experiences designed to challenge traditional notions of ableism.

The inclusion of the LifePrep students on campus is largely supported by a thriving mentor program. With opportunities to learn alongside, socialize, and support the LifePrep students, mentors are involved in almost every aspect of the LifePrep students' day. The LifePrep Mentor Program provides Nazareth students with approximately 6,500 hours of formal engagement yearly and is supported by an operational budget and federal work-study funding.

Mentor roles are carefully constructed to break down the barriers and hierarchy in relationships built through a paid position; it is vital that mentors view the LifePrep students as their peers and through a lens of competence rather than one of deficit.

The program does this through comprehensive training and critical reflection, holding between six to eight mentor training and workshop sessions each year where mentors are engaged in exploring the following: (1) ethics, (2) social positioning, (3) dignity, (4) social competence, (5) supports that lead to independence, and (6) self-advocacy for the mentees.

Mentors also learn about the social foundations of disability and ways to support people with disabilities from a strength-based perspective. Mentors engage in reflective practice throughout the workshops, and topics and exercises are grounded in their experience as mentors and their interactions with the community partners. Most mentors continue with the program for three to four years, allowing them to develop and deepen understanding over time.

Both the mentor program and the co-curricular learning experiences involve Nazareth students that have, in one way or another, made a choice to work with individuals with disabilities.

However, there are expanded opportunities for interaction on campus for students who might not seek out these kinds of experiences. Because of the varied ways LifePrep students are included on campus, Nazareth students find themselves participating alongside the LifePrep students in social activities. As Nazareth students, the LifePrep students attend the campus formal, use the library and fitness center, attend sporting events, play intramural sports, join clubs, or participate in any of the opportunities afforded to the Nazareth student body.

There is no formal teaching taking place in these interactions, the students merely find themselves together in an experience on campus where supports for the LifePrep students are designed to appear invisible in order to provide parity among the participants.

These experiences, where Nazareth students engage with LifePrep students on campus based on their shared interests rather than a choice to work with a particular population, provide additional opportunities to challenge the assumptions around ability held by the Nazareth students.

MEASURING IMPACT

The goal of the LifePrep program is to maximize the learning experiences for all students involved. This requires a carefully crafted set of learning objectives, where all three agencies are equal stakeholders. These objectives drive the learning experiences on campus, and the impact of the program is measured in several ways.

LifePrep's person-centered planning has led to successful outcomes. Of the students who have completed LifePrep, 45 percent have sustained employment, and the remainder are involved in additional training programs or engaging in volunteer opportunities within the community.

These results exceed state and national employment data for persons with I/DD. In 2016, the national percentage of employed people with a cognitive disability was 25 percent, and within New York State, it was only 23 percent (Winsor et al., 2018).

LifePrep Program Mentors

Mentors indicate their service to the program led to growth in their understanding of diversity and to view the LifePrep students as more capable than they had anticipated. In their personal statements, mentors repeatedly discussed the program's impact on their ability to build both professional and personal relationships, reflected on positive gains in dispositions, personal skills, and professional knowledge, and expressed growth in their understanding of the issues facing the LifePrep students. Many expressed new or changing career interests.

Rating scale data support these statements, showing students who reported positive changes in several areas including increases concerning: (1) factual knowledge about developmental disabilities, (2) insight on supporting individuals with I/DD, (3) opportunities to apply coursework, (4) positive changes to attitudes towards people with disabilities, (5) likelihood to interact with individuals with disabilities, (6) understanding of the intersections of (dis)ability, diversity, and inclusion, and (7) skills in both advocacy and supporting the advocacy efforts of others.

While longitudinal data collection from our mentors after graduation has just begun, the reported changes in skills and attitudes towards working with diverse populations, particularly people with I/DD, seem to suggest significant growth in challenging traditional notions of ability.

LifePrep and the Larger Student Body

The impact LifePrep students have had on the way Nazareth students see individuals with I/DD can be viewed through the additional inclusive opportunities created by the larger student body. As the LifePrep program footprint has grown on campus, the LifePrep students and their Nazareth student friends have advocated for additional inclusive experiences.

For instance, students recognized that many intramural experiences were often at times when LifePrep students had difficulty getting to campus. In reaction, they created an additional intramural sports experience, open to all Nazareth students, playing kickball or basketball on Saturday afternoons. A new student-led singing group was started for students who love singing but who didn't want to participate in the more serious choral groups on campus.

Additionally, Nazareth students recognized the opportunities offered to the LifePrep students and wanted to extend these opportunities to other people in the community. They created a new student club "Best Buddies," in partnership with an international organization; this club has provided leadership opportunities for both LifePrep and Nazareth students and provides additional social opportunities for individuals with I/DD within the larger community.

Three years ago, an upswell around graduation occurred. Nazareth students and faculty noticed that the LifePrep students were not included in the college-wide commencement each May and successfully advocated for this to change.

The authors have also begun collecting data from the Nazareth peers in courses with LifePrep students. Many peers in these classes reported these experiences positively impacted their view of people with I/DD and, as a result, see them as more capable.

Students reported that seeing students with I/DD in their class helped them be more accepting of others, more accepting of difference, and provided a better understanding of the abilities of individuals with I/DD. With seemingly little disruption to the learning environment came positive changes that reflect not only attitudes towards students with I/DD but to differences in general.

CONCLUSION

LifePrep serves as a model of how a campus-based community partnership, when integrated fully into campus life, can address exclusionary practices and challenge marginalization. Several aspects of the LifePrep program have led to its success and can provide insight for programs with similar goals. Successes include the following: (1) actively challenging bias; (2) leveraging community expertise; and (3) making authentic connections.

The success of LifePrep has not happened simply by placing new students on campus, but instead, it is driven by the empowerment of Nazareth students through critical reflection and development. The mentor program and curricular experiences directly engage students in learning about equity, diversity, and inclusion. This is necessary to help students challenge their own bias and transform the way they see themselves, their role in the larger social system, and the abilities of others.

Community partners provide the opportunity to invite diverse individuals to campus, but success relies on the purposeful engagement organized in both large and small ways between the partners and the campus. Community partners come with their own resources and areas of expertise, and leveraging these resources yields opportunities for coordinated community

impact. Creating spaces on campus for community partners to directly interact and collaborate with students creates richer and more engaging learning
experiences.

Relationships are an essential component of LifePrep. The growth reported
by mentors and other Nazareth students often cited the friendships they made
with the different stakeholders as foundational to their experience. The lived
experience of relationship building over time creates the types of experiences
that can yield long-lasting changes.

The LifePrep program has provided multiple opportunities for Nazareth
College to engage in learning around diversity, equity, ableism, and bias.
What began as a partnership benefiting the LifePrep students and Nazareth
student mentors has now expanded to become a campus-wide initiative
around inclusive practice. The LifePrep program is a community asset, positively impacting the lives of all of its participants and creating opportunities
for a more inclusive society.

REFERENCES

Artiles, A. J., Kozleski, E. B., Trent, S. C., Osher, D., and Ortiz, A. (2010). Justifying
    and explaining disproportionality, 1968–2008: A critique of underlying views of
    culture. *Exceptional Children*, 76(3), 279–99.
Baglieri, S., Bejoian, L. M., Broderick, A. A., Connor, D. J., and Valle, J. (2011).
    [Re]claiming "inclusive education" toward cohesion in educational reform: Dis-
    ability studies unravels the myth of the normal child. *Teachers College Record*,
    113(10), 2122–54.
Ballard, K. (Ed.) (1999). *Inclusive education: International voices on disability and
    justice.* London: Falmer Press.
Bringle, R., and Hatcher, J. (1995). A service learning curriculum for faculty. *Michi-
    gan Journal of Community Service Learning*, 2, 112–22.
Davis, L. J. (1997) Constructing normalcy. In L. J. Davis (Ed.), *The disability studies
    reader* (2nd ed., pp. 9–28). New York: Routledge.
Gutierrez, K. D., and Rogoff, B. (2003). Cultural ways of learning: Individual traits
    or repertoires of practice. *Educational Researcher*, 32(5), 19–25.
Kuh, G. D. (2008) *High impact educational practices: What they are, who has access
    to them, and why they matter.* Washington, DC: Association of American Colleges
    and Universities.
Mitchell, T. D. (2007). Critical service-learning as social justice education: A case
    study of the citizen scholars program. *Equity & Excellence in Education*, 40(2),
    101–12.
Sapon-Shevin, M. (2003) Inclusion: A matter of social justice. *Educational Leader-
    ship, 61*(2), 25-28.

Skrtic, T. M. (1995) *Disability and democracy: Reconstructing (special) education for postmodernity.* New York: Teachers College Press.

Winsor, J., Timmons, J., Butterworth, J., Migliore, A., Domin, D., Zalewska, A., and Shepard, J. (2018). *State data: The national report on employment services and outcomes.* Boston, MA: University of Massachusetts Boston, Institute for Community Inclusion.

Part IV

COMMUNITY ENGAGEMENT

Chapter Ten

A Service-Learning Approach to Equity, Diversity, and Inclusion

Ryan Colwell and Jessica Baldizon

Service learning is a form of experiential, reflective education where community activities support and enhance the learning goals of an academic course (Howard, 1998; Jacoby, 1996). University and community partners collaborate to design service-learning experiences that contribute to the students' learning and meet real community needs (Erickson and Anderson, 1997). Additionally, service learning is a powerful agent for social justice (Payne-Jackson, 2015; Calderón, 2007). Service-learning experiences may help students discover their role in addressing issues of equity, diversity, and inclusion (EDI) within community settings.

This chapter begins with an introduction to a university literacy methods course sequence and the diverse, urban school in which the courses were embedded as a service-learning component. The authors then discuss how four critical service-learning practices empowered university and community partners to address issues of EDI and indicate how these practices are applicable across disciplines. These practices include: (1) relationship-building; (2) challenging preexisting ideas and beliefs; (3) blending content and experiential learning opportunities; and (4) engaging in assessment, reflection, and goal setting.

THE LITERACY METHODS COURSE
SEQUENCE AT CHASE SCHOOL

Throughout the 2017–2018 academic year, an elementary education professor and his students spent Monday mornings at Chase School (a pseudonym) as part of a two-semester literacy methods course sequence. The elementary candidates were all seniors, enrolled in a five-year, integrated, bachelor's/

master's teacher-preparation program at a small, predominately white, Jesuit university in the Northeastern United States.

During the fall semester, the college students took "Developing Literacy in the Elementary School," a course that explored how students from kindergarten to second grade learn to read, write, listen, speak, view, and engage in critical thinking. In the spring semester, students took "Extending Literacy in the Elementary School," a course that explored the continuation of literacy development and learning in grades three through six.

Chase is a local pre-K-to-eighth-grade school, which is located in an urban school district near the university. The student population at Chase is culturally and linguistically diverse, and the majority of the students at the school were eligible for free-or-reduced-price meals. This partnership between a predominantly white university and a diverse experiential learning site was selected, in part, to engage future elementary school teachers in issues of EDI as a core component of their teacher preparation program.

On a weekly basis during the 2017–2018 school year, the professor and his elementary candidates met in a classroom at Chase School for their literacy methods coursework. They spent ninety minutes together as a class, and then the elementary candidates spent sixty minutes completing service learning in classrooms during a reading/writing block. This block was chosen in consultation with Chase administration and faculty.

RELATIONSHIP-BUILDING

Relationship-building has been identified as a cornerstone of any service-learning collaboration between university and community partners (Stoecker, 2016). Both university and community partners must get to know one another, determine the strengths and challenges that they bring to the learning experience, and establish shared goals that they believe will provide reciprocal benefits for everyone involved (Ngai, Cheung, Ngai, and Chan, 2009). These relationship-building experiences are critical as they raise important issues of EDI that can be addressed as a service-learning course is designed and carried out.

The Service Learning Coordinator at Chase School (and co-author of this chapter) played an important role in supporting this relationship-building process. She organized a meeting with the professor, the administrators, and the teachers at Chase who expressed interest in the program. As an outcome of this initial meeting, the professor and the classroom teachers co-constructed course-learning goals and assignments that aligned with the content of the university coursework and the literacy learning needs of the teachers and students at Chase.

When the academic year began at Chase School, the professor, his elementary education candidates, and the administration, teachers, and students at Chase engaged in other activities designed to establish a strong and trusting relationship.

The principal of Chase visited the literacy methods class to welcome the professor and elementary candidates to his school and share context about the community. The principal discussed strengths, such as classroom teachers celebrating their students' cultural assets by inviting students and their family members to share their cultural stories and traditions, and then weaving those stories and traditions into the classroom curriculum.

The principal also candidly shared some of the challenges faced by the students, faculty, and Chase school community, such as limited resources, large class sizes, lack of faculty diversity, and limited support staff (e.g., paraprofessionals, school psychologists, school nurses, substitute teachers, etc.).

This led to a discussion among the professor and his students about their own strengths and challenges that they brought to the partnership. The professor identified as a strength that the university library had a broad teaching collection of children's books and other literacy materials available to his students. One of the elementary candidates noted that a challenge for her would be to learn new teaching strategies that were effective with English language learners (ELL), who made up more than 40 percent of the student body at Chase School.

The Chase Service Learning Coordinator described how a commitment to building relationships was of paramount importance when she wrote in a reflection:

> Instead of immediately jumping to "solutions" as outsiders, the professor and his students truly worked to gain trust and build knowledge of the school community first. This commitment to relationships is what has allowed the Chase administration and faculty to be welcoming and willing to engage in the collaboration.

While this example of relationship-building is specific to the literacy course sequence, university instructors from any discipline can benefit from the techniques of communication, reflection, collaboration, and open dialogue that characterize this partnership.

CHALLENGING PREEXISTING IDEAS AND BELIEFS

One of the benefits of service-learning collaborations between university and community partners is that they may include experiences that challenge participants' preexisting ideas and beliefs (Calderón, 2007). However, if service-learning collaborations are ineffective, they can also reinforce stereotypes or various forms of privilege (Butin, 2006). Service-learning course assignments offer one reflective space where students can explore and challenge their own preexisting ideas and beliefs, particularly regarding issues of EDI.

Early in the fall semester at Chase School, the professor asked his students to create an autobiography, in which they shared their own histories as readers and writers (Graves, 1994). Elementary candidates told stories about how they learned to read and write, who their best literacy teachers were growing up, what educational lessons/resources helped them the most, and what challenges they faced.

After developing their autobiographies, elementary candidates then developed a literacy interview protocol to find out who the students at Chase were as readers and writers. Students brainstormed general background questions (e.g., "How did you learn to read/write?," "Who helped you learn how to read/write?," etc.); questions about students' literacy interests (e.g., "Who is your favorite author?," "What topics do you like to write about?," etc.); and questions about students' literacy beliefs and goals (e.g., "What do you think you do well as a reader?," "How would you like to improve as a writer?," etc.).

Elementary candidates conducted a literacy interview with one of the students in their service-learning classrooms, analyzed the results, and developed biographies of their Chase students. Although this assignment was particular to literacy, the concept is transferable across content areas. Professors can work with students and community partners to reflect on a common set of questions in the interest of developing an awareness of preexisting beliefs.

When the elementary candidates returned to class to share the biographies of their Chase students, they noticed similarities between their own reading/writing histories and the reading/writing histories of the students they interviewed. For example, several elementary candidates shared a favorite genre of reading or writing with the students that they interviewed at Chase.

However, the elementary candidates also identified substantial differences between their own reading/writing histories and the reading/writing histories of the students at Chase. In their autobiographies, several elementary candidates discussed the rich literacy resources they had as children, such as a large collection of books to read both at school and at home. During their interviews, students at Chase wished that they could have more books in their classrooms and at home, including books with more diverse characters.

By autobiographically delving into their own histories as readers and writers, and then exploring the reading/writing experiences of the students at Chase

School, elementary candidates challenged preexisting ideas and beliefs about teaching and learning. They discovered that individuals have different learning styles and interests, develop their own personal strengths, and face their own personal challenges as they learn how to read and write. Further, experiences of learning how to read and write are unique and not always equitable.

The Service Learning Coordinator noted that Chase classroom teachers sought to help elementary candidates challenge their assumptions surrounding teaching and learning, particularly in an urban setting. Without deliberately questioning what it means to be a reader/writer and how one's own literacy experiences shape these views, teachers run the risk of teaching students without facilitating learning. By collaborating with Chase teachers, elementary candidates had an opportunity to build an awareness of self and others, while Chase faculty made explicit what it means and looks like to teach for EDI in their school.

BLENDING CONTENT AND EXPERIENTIAL LEARNING OPPORTUNITIES

Students engaged in service-learning courses develop knowledge and skills in a particular content area, and they can immediately apply their knowledge and skills within the context of their service learning (Davidson, Jimenez, Onifade, and Hankins, 2010).

A purposeful blend of content and experiential learning opportunities provides a space in which university faculty can engage students in culturally responsive teaching and learning, and students can immediately take action to pursue EDI in the communities in which they are embedded. While the skills we discuss below are particular to our learning experience, we will indicate how they are transferable.

A major goal of the literacy methods course sequence at Chase School was to help elementary candidates develop and practice the pedagogical skills that would empower them to be effective K–6 teachers of reading and writing.

The professor and his elementary candidates explored research-based teaching strategies throughout the academic year. The elementary candidates were then invited to apply their new teaching skills during their service-learning hours in Chase classrooms. Given the cultural and linguistic diversity of the students at Chase, it was crucial for the university professor and his elementary candidates to explore, discuss, and implement culturally responsive teaching.

Further, the authors believe that any learning experience that involves similar demographics as ours must address culturally competent teaching and interacting—even if the college students are not future teachers. Skills and activities from education can be widely applied across disciplines.

One of the first literacy skills that the professor introduced to his elementary candidates was the practice of activating students' background knowledge about a text's author, setting, topic, genre, or characters before reading. In groups, the elementary candidates were given a piece of children's literature to read and asked to think about how they would activate students' background knowledge regarding their specific text.

One group of elementary candidates discussed Cynthia Rylant's (1985) picture book, *The Relatives Came*, which tells the story of a family reunion. Among their ideas for activating students' background knowledge was to ask elementary students to share examples of what happens when their own families get together.

After the elementary candidates shared their teaching strategies for helping students activate background knowledge, the professor then asked his students to think specifically about the students at Chase School and consider potential barriers that could get in the way of activating background knowledge.

One group of elementary candidates noted that if a teacher was reading a story about hiking in the mountains, students raised exclusively in an urban setting may never have gone hiking before and have no background knowledge to activate.

Professors from many disciplines who send students into community experiences can benefit from thinking through how background knowledge, which overlaps with cultural difference, affects understanding for both their college students and community members.

As they developed their biographies of the readers and writers at Chase, many of the elementary candidates learned that the Chase students wanted to read books that had more diverse characters in them that reflected their own identities.

In response, the professor and his students explored strategies for identifying and integrating multicultural children's literature into classroom reading and writing instruction. Teaching strategies included using multicultural children's literature to challenge cultural stereotypes, examining events from multiple perspectives, and highlighting diverse cultural beliefs and experiences (Gopalakrishnan, 2011).

Although learning and applying culturally-responsive teaching strategies is specific to training teacher candidates, college professors from many disciplines, and college students, in general, can also benefit from reflecting on these strategies. It is not just diverse elementary students who benefit from seeing their identities, or the identities of others with whom they are not familiar, reflected in the curriculum. This speaks to the need for an inclusive curriculum throughout higher education.

ENGAGING IN ASSESSMENT, REFLECTION, AND GOAL SETTING

To develop and sustain long-lasting partnerships, there needs to be an ongoing assessment of the partnership, with opportunities for reflection and goal setting from all stakeholders (Holland, 2001). One of the most important outcomes of this cycle of assessment, reflection, and goal setting is that university and community partners can commit to ongoing improvement as they pursue issues of EDI.

As the first year of the literacy course sequence wrapped up at Chase School, the professor asked his elementary candidates to engage in both oral and written reflection activities. Students discussed the benefits and challenges of engaging in service learning and considered how their service learning impacted who they are, or will become, as future elementary school teachers. In their reflections, many of the elementary candidates mentioned the benefits of "moving outside their comfort zone" and "gaining valuable experiences" in a culturally and linguistically diverse school setting.

The elementary candidates also described a number of challenges, such as meeting the needs of English language learners at Chase, when the candidates had never been second-language learners themselves. Elementary candidates also noted the challenge of limited instructional resources at Chase School. One candidate completed her service learning in a bilingual classroom where there simply weren't enough bilingual texts for students to read.

As part of the service-learning partnership, teachers at Chase School were also asked to engage in assessment and reflection surveys, providing their thoughts about having elementary candidates visit their classrooms to support reading and writing instruction. With limited support staff available at Chase, many of the teachers were thrilled to have elementary candidates in their classrooms.

One teacher discussed how the elementary candidates enabled her to run differentiated literacy centers, which helped her to engage in valuable small group instruction. Another teacher felt that her students benefited from the one-on-one time that they got to spend with the elementary candidates.

The teachers at Chase also brainstormed about how the service-learning partnership could be improved. The teachers wanted more communication about what to expect from the elementary candidates when they visited on a weekly basis.

They also suggested that the elementary candidates' course assignments could more strongly align with the existing reading and writing curriculum at Chase. A number of teachers at Chase asked if the elementary candidates could help to support the reading and writing intervention process at Chase, since the school did not always have budgetary funds available to hire reading and writing interventionists as part of their full-time faculty.

By engaging university and community stakeholders in assessment and reflection regarding their service-learning partnerships, professors can set collaborative goals to improve their partnerships moving forward.

CONCLUSION

Service learning can be a powerful vehicle through which faculty and students can collaborate with community partners to pursue shared goals. The authors recommend that university faculty, students, and community partners engage in four critical service-learning practices and that these learning practices can be applied across academic disciplines.

REFERENCES

Butin, D. W. (2006). The limits of service learning in higher education. *The Review of Higher Education*, 29(4), 473–98.

Calderón, J. (2007). *Race, poverty, and social justice: Multidisciplinary perspectives through service learning.* Sterling, VA: Stylus Publishing.

Davidson, W., Jimenez, T., Onifade, E., and Hankins, S. (2010). Student experiences of the adolescent diversion project: A community-based exemplar in the pedagogy of service-learning. *American Journal of Community Psychology*, 46(3–4), 442–58.

Erickson, J., and Anderson, J. (1997). *Learning with the community: Concepts and models for service-learning in teacher education.* Washington, DC: American Association for Higher Education.

Gopalakrishnan, A. (2011). *Multicultural children's literature: A critical issues approach.* Thousand Oaks, CA: Sage.

Graves, D. (1994). *A fresh look at writing.* Portsmouth, NH: Heinemann.

Holland, B. (2001). A comprehensive model for assessing service-learning and community-university partnerships. *New Directions for Higher Education, 2001*(114), 51–60.

Howard, J. P. F. (1998). Academic service learning: A counternormative pedagogy. *New Directions for Teaching and Learning*, 21–29.

Jacoby, B. (1996). *Service-learning in higher education: Concepts and practice.* San Francisco, CA: Jossey-Bass.

Ngai, S. Y., Cheung, C. K., Ngai, N. P., and Chan, K. B. (2009). Building reciprocal partnerships for service-learning: The experiences of Hong Kong secondary school teachers. *Child & Youth Services*, 31, 170–87.

Payne-Jackson, A. (2015). *Service learning: An agent for social change.* Palo Alto, CA: Academica Press.

Rylant, C. (1985). *The relatives came.* New York: Bradbury Press.

Stoecker, R. (2016). *Liberating service learning and the rest of higher education civic engagement.* Philadelphia: Temple University Press.

Chapter Eleven

Using Interdisciplinary Intersections to Promote Equity, Diversity, and Inclusion

Sarah K. Donovan and Margarita Sánchez

This chapter offers strategies and practices for utilizing experiential learning, broadly defined, to integrate disciplines while embedding equity, diversity, and inclusion (EDI) into the curriculum. It begins with a description of how a learning community at Wagner College that combines the disciplines of Spanish and philosophy developed a community project to connect the disciplines and advance EDI goals. Based on this example, the authors identify and describe four general strategies and practices that worked in their learning community and indicate how they are applicable across or between many disciplines.

INTERDISCIPLINARY, EXPERIENTIAL, AND EDI GOALS

Wagner College is a small, private, liberal arts college in Staten Island, New York City, with an academic and civic engagement agenda. The student population is predominantly white with a sizeable commuter population. Staten Island itself is historically predominantly white and is known politically as the red borough (Barron, 2018). It is also home to rising immigrant populations. All first-year students begin their college career in a learning community comprised of three courses that are taught from an interdisciplinary perspective. Students also participate in twenty hours of experiential learning connected to the learning community.

In the learning community that serves as the example of this chapter, all students take intermediate Spanish with Professor Sánchez and a philosophy course on contemporary moral problems with Professor Donovan. The third course is co-taught by Sánchez and Donovan, and it is a writing-intensive course in which students reflect on their experiential learning, the connection between the disciplines, and the EDI goals.

For this particular learning community, the EDI goals are to encourage students to reflect on the constructed nature of linguistic, racial and ethnic identity, and the moral dimensions of social categories, all as they explore Spanish culture and diverse ethical theories.

While this model has three courses, the authors have taught in other interdisciplinary learning communities with two independent courses, or one team-taught, and were able to achieve modified EDI goals—sometimes without a robust experiential learning component. While it is always ideal to have more contact with the students and each other, as well as an experience that makes the goals more palpable, communication between professors engaged with EDI goals that result in intentionality with the syllabus and lectures can also be highly effective.

The community project for this learning community was located in an immigrant center in Port Richmond, Staten Island, near the professors' campus. Port Richmond is home to a growing immigrant population primarily from Mexico and Central America. Each step of the planning process involved community activist and non-profit director Gonzalo Mercado and a Wagner student who was his intern. As the professors worked with the community leaders and members to develop and run an after-school tutoring program for immigrant children, they thought through how to construct ethical community relationships (Donovan, 2017).

While this chapter uses the Spanish and philosophy learning community as an example, it is important to note that many of the twenty-plus learning communities offered every fall at Wagner College have adapted their discipline-specific courses and EDI goals to experiential components in similar local communities—without a language component.

For example, Professors Alison Arant, from the English department, and Patricia Moynagh, from Government and Politics, developed community projects with a local Liberian community in Park Hill. Part of their course focuses on the history of Liberian immigration and civil war and includes a meeting with a scholar who studies the local community. Students then participate in literacy and cultural events at the immigrant center.

PROMOTING INTERDISCIPLINARY THINKING AND EDI

Professors Sánchez and Donovan worked in the Port Richmond community over many years as they developed strategies and practices for creating meaningful experiences that promoted interdisciplinary thinking and EDI goals. This section describes the following strategies and practices, borne out of this collaboration, and indicates where they might be broadly applicable: working across disciplines with EDI goals, reflecting on the self, actively observing, and reflecting on the other.

Working Across Disciplines with EDI Goals

Combining disciplines that are different from each other works well for interdisciplinary and EDI goals if the professors are able to clearly articulate points of intersection. With the Spanish and philosophy learning community, the professors identified the importance of challenging the view that language courses are only practical, skill-based courses, and philosophy courses are only abstract. They utilized experiential learning and the EDI goals to challenge preconceptions about the disciplines and to connect them. This section demonstrates how the professors achieved this and suggests how this can be done with other disciplines.

A foreign language—in this case, Spanish—is a valuable skill that must be learned through repetition, memorization, and practice. However, students don't always see the philosophical and moral dimensions of language. Intellectuals from diverse traditions have focused on these dimensions. From the structural linguistics of Ferdinand de Saussure, to Jacques Derrida's deconstruction, to Wittgenstein's perspective on rule-following and private language, intellectuals have explored the constructed nature and opacity of language. Learning a foreign language along with philosophy helps students reflect on the philosophical dimensions of language.

One example from the Spanish and philosophy learning community encourages students to focus on how language influences their view of themselves or their identity. Professor Sánchez rarely speaks English with the students in her Spanish class. She prompts conversations in Spanish through the creative design of exercises that allow them to act out roles and feel less self-conscious. She balances students feeling alienated with learning skills to address it. This primes students for empathy as they experience what it is like to be on the outside (unable to communicate) and how to overcome it by developing their language skills.

When her students then engage with immigrant communities, they are prepared. They walk into a different linguistic and cultural environment, and they are unable to break the linguistic barrier by pulling the conversation back to English. For many students, they experience not being understood, not feeling like they belong, and, in effect, not feeling like themselves. But their Spanish, however limited, is their toolkit for countering the alienation;

they experience how identity is bound to language. Experiences such as these can prime students for discussions about connections between different disciplines and for conversations about EDI concepts.

To help students think through complex questions about identity, how it is constructed in a social and linguistic context, and how many forms of communication have a moral dimension, Professor Donovan introduces a different skill set and presents it as practical. The students learn a common vocabulary, based on a spectrum of moral theories, that allows them to articulate their moral belief system. Understanding their own beliefs and the range of alternate belief systems gives students the tools they need to articulate and think critically about what they are experiencing at the immigrant center.

With a clear idea of the existing interdisciplinarity, the professors ask students to reflect on—usually first in small written assignments, and then in class discussions—the larger philosophical questions about linguistic identity that their experience at the immigrant center raises, such as: "When you became aware of failures of communication, how did it affect your confidence in continuing with the conversation? Were you self-conscious about your identity at that moment? How did you feel once you entered back into your linguistic comfort zone? How did this make you reflect on your human relationships in general?"

These reflections help students recognize and respect that immigrants are able to present themselves as full, complex subjects within their own linguistic and cultural realm but have difficulty navigating an English-speaking world. It also serves as a bridge to discussing the racial and ethnic identity of the immigrants.

While this example is specific to this learning community, the idea of searching for that central point of interdisciplinary intersection, articulating it so that students can understand it, and utilizing EDI to promote the learning has been replicated across disciplines at the same institution—without teaching students a foreign language. Other learning communities similarly pay careful attention to the value each discipline brings to the table and how an experience can help to magnify interdisciplinary and EDI goals.

For example, other learning communities in the sciences and social sciences have students read about and discuss environmental hazards in public parks where children play and how and why disinvested communities are more likely to face these issues. The experiential component includes testing water in local communities. Nursing students learn about the limited access to health for undocumented workers and how that is both a public health and a moral issue. They participate in raising awareness about a health issue at a local clinic.

Even without off-campus experiential learning, professors can utilize interdisciplinary teaching and an experience to achieve EDI goals. Professor

Racquel DeCicco, Chemistry, and Professor Celeste Gagnon, Anthropology, co-teach a course in which they connect the chemical components of food with their origins and cultural importance. For a final project, students work with a partner to research the origins of a dish—such as falafel, borscht, or hamburgers—and the social, political, or economic issues related to it. They develop and share presentations with the class.

Reflecting on the Self

An important way to begin the experiential learning is for professors to observe first-hand their students' initial reactions to the experiential learning site. In the Spanish and philosophy learning community, the professors accompany the students on a walking tour of Port Richmond, along with a group visit to the immigrant center. At the site, the students typically meet with the director, who takes time to discuss the population with whom the students will be working. This gives the professors a chance to get to know their students and to observe their reactions to the neighborhood.

In the case of the Spanish and philosophy learning community, students often appear to be self-conscious when they enter the immigrant center for the first time. While all students may appear self-conscious, students typically feel self-conscious for different reasons.

At a predominantly white institution where faculty and students are working with a community of color, it is particularly important for professors to anticipate the complex ethical and moral dimensions that they might be creating for their students of color (Mitchell and Donahue, 2009; Mitchell, Donahue, and Young-Law, 2012; Bocci, 2015). During the first visit, the professors encourage students to practice self-reflection.

The first classroom discussion after the trip to the community gives students a space in which to juxtapose what they have heard, or even read, about Port Richmond with the friendly and welcoming environment of the immigrant center. Students are not always forthcoming, so the authors have also asked students to write down an anonymous comment or question on a piece of paper that is collected at the beginning of class.

Drawing out cognitive dissonance is a great starting point for students. The dissonance typically grows as students begin to form bonds at the immigrant center, to think critically and ethically about the social problems they are seeing, and develop an identity in Spanish.

Actively Observing

Wagner students enter learning communities with many assumptions influenced by their positionality regarding race, ethnicity, native language, economic class, and education, to name a few. An important intervention is for instructors to encourage students to be active observers about their everyday environment.

This type of investigation is not foreign to them. As professional students, they have been asked to be critical thinkers, readers, and observers in the classroom regarding their textbooks, papers, and exams. In the Spanish and philosophy learning community, the professors saw an opportunity to use two simple exercises to teach students how to transfer these important academic skills to daily living in order to move from active learners to active observers.

One way to encourage active observation that is appropriate throughout a semester is to discuss the importance of the words we use to describe what we see (e.g., ask students to reflect on why they use the word "weird" to describe something that is new). In this learning community, both discipline-specific courses are focused on the importance of precise language, but language and vocabulary are important to any academic discipline.

This learning community emphasizes how language is linked to culture and history, and students start to recognize some interesting distinctions: In English, we "make a decision," while in Spanish, we "take a decision" (*tomar una decisión*). In Spanish, there is a whole list of "no fault" verbs: you don't lose something, it gets lost (*"se me perdió"*). In these examples, the speaker has a completely different relationship to the object than in English. Thus, a foreign language can be disorienting not only because of the new words but also because of the new relationships that must be learned.

While here we are talking quite literally about a foreign language, every discipline has a specialized vocabulary and methodology that it uses to approach the world, which may feel foreign to students. Professors can make an effort to connect the worldviews that they are teaching to specific community experiences, pointing out when a discipline's specific methodology might not work because of an epistemic prejudice.

A second example is a digital storytelling project in which students become active observers behind a camera lens as they take pictures in the Port Richmond community. They use these to create a short, three-to-five-minute, narrated video that tells their story about this community. This can be modified by simply having them take pictures to analyze in class. In this learning community, part of the assignment is for students to find creative and artistic ways to represent complex ideas through pictures without showing the faces of immigrants who may not be documented; this works as a general practice.

Reflecting on Difference

Students become ready to reflect on difference in the Spanish and philosophy learning community in three steps that have broad applicability. First, by learning a foreign language and meeting immigrants, they confront their entrenchment in their own culture. However, even without learning a new language, students could still be guided by professors to see cultural entrenchment. For example, the learning community between English and Government and Politics that focuses on the Liberian community addresses cultural difference without a language component.

Second, by engaging in the community, students have consistent experiences of being the linguistic outsider. While the language difference overtly facilitates this, many traditional-aged students experience alienation just by engaging in any experience that feels remotely new to them. Even without a community experience, this is possible. In the example of the Anthropology and Chemistry professor, students are thrown off-kilter by being asked to engage with the food they eat as chemical formulas and cultural artifacts.

Third, by working with individuals at the immigrant center, students must think about people with a different cultural background and belief system with whom they otherwise might not have crossed paths. This can happen with or without the language component. An example from the Spanish and philosophy learning community demonstrates a telling shift in perspective that occurred through the work at the after-school tutoring program.

When students work with children, those children's parents are often sitting in the background. The college students begin to realize that the parents are there because they would desperately like to help their children with their homework, but they lack the English-language skills.

Wagner students begin to understand that, in the act of tutoring a child, they are helping to bridge two worlds. For many of them, this is a meaningful, ethical experience. This type of experience is not unique to the Spanish and philosophy learning community but could happen in any experience that primes students to think broadly, reflect on themselves, and engage thoughtfully with EDI topics.

CONCLUSION

As the semester progresses, students are encouraged to transition from thinking of their work in the community solely concerning how they are helping the community. They also think about how the community has helped them— often with minimal prompting. This moves them away from a negative model of a one-way service relationship and reinforces EDI goals.

This work has also been personally and professionally rewarding for the faculty in the Spanish and philosophy learning community. Both have become more deeply involved in projects in the Port Richmond community as a result of this work, and they have made it an integral part of their research (Sánchez, 2016; McNair, Donovan, and Siegel, 2017). Both maintain that faculty working across disciplines, with experiential learning, and for EDI goals, fundamentally alter their relationship with their discipline in creative and fruitful ways that can facilitate change in academia as a whole.

REFERENCES

Barron, S. (December 2018). New York's red borough. *City Journal*. Retrieved from https://www.city-journal.org/html/new-yorks-red-borough-15652.html.

Bocci, M. (2015). Community-based learning and white normativity: Racial representation in community-based learning's historical narrative. *Michigan Journal of Community Service Learning*, 22(1), 5–17. http://hdl.handle.net/2027/spo .3239521.0022.101.

Donovan, S. (2017). Challenging privilege in community-based learning and in the Philosophy classroom. *AAPT Studies in Pedagogy*, 3, 129–53. doi:10.5840/aapt studies201712431.

McNair, L., Donovan S., and Siegel, S. (2017). Work that matters: Preparing future leaders from vulnerable communities. In N. Aloni and L. Weintrob (Eds.), *Beyond Bystanders: Educational Leadership for a Humane Culture in a Globalizing Reality* (pp. 233–44). New York: Sense Publishers.

Mitchell, T. D., and Donahue, D. M. (2009). 'I do more service in this class than I ever do at my site': Paying attention to the reflections of students of color in service learning. In J. R. Strait and M. Lima (Eds.), *The Future of Community-based Learning: New Solutions for Sustaining and Improving Practice* (pp. 172–90). Sterling, VA: Stylus.

Mitchell, T. D., Donahue, D. M., and Young-Law, C. (2012). Community-based learning as a pedagogy of whiteness. *Equity and Excellence in Education*, 45(4), 612–29. https://doi.org/10.1080/10665684.2012.715534.

Sánchez, M. (2016). Thinking transnational: The reunification of migrant families. In K. Gonzalez and R. Frumkin (Eds.), *Handbook of Research on Effective Communication in Culturally Diverse Classrooms* (pp. 230–50). Hershey, PA: IGI Global https://doi.org/10.4018/978-1-4666-9953-3.ch012.

Part V

FIRST-PERSON NARRATIVE

Chapter Twelve

The Personal as Transformative in the Liberal Arts Classroom

Heather Finch, Shelby Longard, and
Amy Hodges Hamilton

College students are eager to address the inequities of race, class, and gender; therefore, teachers must be prepared to shepherd them through the process. As bell hooks describes in *Teaching to Transgress,* engaged pedagogy, "does not seek simply to empower students" but also creates a space "where teachers grow, and are empowered by the process" (1994, p. 21). In this collaborative chapter, three professors will examine the ways interdisciplinary teaching, writing, and rhetoric may open up spaces to empower students and teachers through autobiography in the classroom community.

The personal can offer an important lens through which faculty and students alike shape the classroom space in meaningful and impactful ways. Through conscious vulnerability—sharing pieces of themselves in both the curriculum and pedagogy—instructors can change the way their students experience equity, diversity, and inclusion (EDI) concerns.

MOVING THE PERSONAL INTO THE
MODERN COLLEGE CLASSROOM

Personal experience is central in Paulo Freire's (1970) *Pedagogy of the Oppressed.* This work stems from Freire's observations of marginalization from his own childhood of extreme poverty and social mistreatment; indeed, experiential learning stands as the foundation of his teachings. The first stage of Freire's *Pedagogy* is the consciousness of those in question: The oppressed and oppressor alike must develop an understanding of themselves and their situation (1970, p. 55).

He later argues the importance of multiple frameworks and examination of all oppression, a form of intersectionality introduced well before its more recent and popular iterations. This intersectionality is an important development within the modern university classroom, but it can also become problematic when misused. As Freire and his contemporaries posit, it is not enough to explain and quantify the nature of poverty or racism or sexism or heterosexism—a cause and, indeed, an oppressor must be named, as well as a course of action. Pedagogy must be transformative in nature.

Inspired by Freire's work and her lived experience, bell hooks (1994) similarly reflects on her educational journey in *Teaching to Transgress*, where she details how her racial, class, and gender identity impact learning and classroom experiences. hooks urges teachers to "serve as [the] catalyst that calls everyone to become more and more engaged, to become active participants in learning" (1994, p. 11).

In an increasingly diverse classroom, it is paramount for teachers to "teach in ways that transform consciousness, creating a climate of free expression" (hooks, 1994, p. 44). When teachers share this willingness and freedom with students, they contribute to the creation of knowledge through shared personal experience.

Patricia Hill Collins's (2000) consideration of black women's lived experiences offers a critical review of epistemological standards and argues that lived experience, particularly among the marginalized, stands as credible evidence even when undervalued by the majority. In her work, *Black Feminist Thought*, she recognizes alternative epistemologies and considers the "emphasis placed on individual uniqueness" as an integral part of knowledge creation (Hill Collins, 2000, p. 263).

In the face of current divisive shifts in modern politics and the economy, teaching young people about the interrelated nature of race, class, and gender—as well as the oppression and privilege that stem from them—has become an increasingly delicate balancing act. Many students—particularly those who benefit from the status quo—find the sterile approach of academic inquiry to be personally threatening and are reluctant to heed the lessons therein. This personal hesitance, combined with an increased skepticism of the presumed liberal academic agenda, makes even the simplest lessons on injustice hard to absorb.

When students have little personal familiarity with oppression, it is difficult to imagine the realities of marginalized groups and perceive one's own complicity. On the other hand, students whose own lives reflect those difficulties often experience a more complex and sometimes exploitative dynamic within such a classroom.

The ways in which teachers and their students mediate uncomfortable classroom spaces will not only determine learning outcomes but will also determine how students move that learning outside of the classroom. While it is a more difficult path, teachers who choose to embrace the uncomfortable, humble themselves through personal reflection and admission of social location, and cede ownership of the learning space to their students may see learning enriched and find themselves among those most impacted by the outcome.

As Freire and others have noted, bringing the personal into play must be transformative in nature. Each author models autobiographical storytelling in one of the next three sections to create a radical pedagogy and become "vulnerable while encouraging students to take risks" (hooks, 1994, p. 21) by breaking the academic third person intentionally.

Finch: Centering Race in the Classroom

My first encounters with pedagogies of race and their impact on epistemology began as an undergraduate student at a Historically Black College/University (HBCU). My fellow students represented an array of cultures and national identities of the African diaspora, and the instructors' racial and ethnic identities represented the world. While I did not have the language or experience of a teacher at the time, I recognized the high expectations for students to learn in engaging ways at high levels on uncomfortable topics, many related to oppression.

As I transitioned to the classroom as a teacher in a predominately white institution, I immediately became aware of how my race and gender impacted my students' perceptions of me as well as my pedagogy. I realized quickly that I cannot deny I am a black woman. Both my race and gender intersect with the work that I do and the ways students interact with me and the topic of freedom. One class of twenty-five students consisted of only one student of color—a Nigerian American.

The first day he sat in the very last row in the corner by himself. This visual reminder of racial underrepresentation took me by surprise, and he reacted similarly. While this student remained silent through most class discussions, he visited me more than any other student during office hours, wanting to know more about my personal experiences at my undergraduate institution. I did not immediately understand what my personal stories could offer him, but he always wanted to know more.

Through this experience, I had the epiphany to learn how to create a class community with discussions, spaces, and techniques that promoted and encouraged an equitable and diverse experience that included personal stories. This required my vulnerability as I shared my own personal stories of racial and gender discrimination.

One distinctive moment in the classroom occurred when we covered black women's responses to experiencing freedom as part of families. As we discussed Claudia Rankine's "The Condition of Black Life is One of Mourning" (2016), space opened for me to share how I navigate a world where my race shapes perceptions and reactions from a world where the narrative privileges white skin.

We reviewed the absurd rite of passage that requires the "talk"—a solemn and scary conversation where parents' fears rise as they outline what should happen if you are stopped by the police, you want to shop in a store with "high-end" items, or you are gathering with friends in your "affluent" neighborhood. I looked at my class of nineteen with two black students and one Indian student and shared how my parents had the "talk" with me and how, even in my adult years, it impacted how I responded to being stopped by a police officer in my "affluent" neighborhood.

As I recounted how imperative it was for me to ask the officer's permission before every movement to make sure I lived, the classroom became silent. At this moment, we moved from the page where Rankine described the experiences of those from national headlines to our classroom, where our own lived experiences became credible evidence (Hill Collins, 2000).

Intentionally sharing stories such as these made it apparent that many students also desired to engage in similar ways. The vulnerability it takes to ask the deeper questions and respond with the personal experiences became part of the courses' main vein. The fruitful conversation brought in the many layers of challenges and commentary when working to build an equitable, diverse, and inclusive classroom community.

Longard: The Relevance of Stories in Social Science

Across a decade of teaching sociology, my pedagogy has evolved. Together with these stylistic adaptations, my relationships with students and the material I teach has also shifted. One semester after the other, I share more of myself with the material. Pieces of my own autobiography give context and broader depth; personal testimony fleshes out larger societal patterns. Sociological concepts, demographic trends, and statistical charts are one thing; the lived experiences of a faculty member willing to share them are quite another.

Sociologists teach the "uncomfortable" stuff—topics the dominant group conditioned students avoid. As a result, students often have difficulty seeing the personal within the social. Our personal experiences are tied up in the public issues that face our society. And as our society shifts and conversations regarding inequity become more contentious, students are increasingly reluctant to discuss our societal problems.

For years, I simply taught the facts, putting the hard math on the projector. I hoped the lessons would stick. When the facts diverged from what students had learned at home or in the media, I crossed my fingers and hoped science would win out. However, over time, I have found it more instructive to give my students pieces of my story. When faculty are "real" with their students, they extend a form of respect that facilitates learning. Students are gifted with the freedom to learn not just from science but from experience and testimony.

To humble oneself in front of students is difficult. When I recount the realities of my childhood poverty, it rips away the armor of status. Students are puzzled to see the intricacies and nuances become real in their professor, who becomes a person as the material becomes more than a chart.

In my classroom, I teach both poverty and white privilege with self as case studies. As a feminist trained in standpoint theory, I embrace my experience as a woman whose childhood was marked by poverty (Harding, 1986, 1991). However, it is more complex than that. I talk of a childhood steeped in hunger but girded by whiteness. Pulling from Hill Collins's *Black Feminist Thought* (2000), I assert my own limitations in experience.

My struggles enhance my comprehension and understanding of social class, but my whiteness limits my standpoint regarding racial oppression. One of the hardest lessons to teach is intersectionality—white students, in particular, have trouble seeing themselves as somehow categorically more privileged than others. This is especially difficult for whites who have struggled financially or whose ancestors were impoverished. However, student assumptions about what privilege *must* look like are challenged when the nuance of supremacy is brought to light.

When teachers admit their own structural complicity within the confines of an unequal society, students have less to fear from acknowledging their own place within it. This takes constant self-assessment; those committed to the fight against oppression must "re-examine themselves constantly" (Freire, 1970, p. 60). So I give them pieces of my life. I tell them about my single mom and her struggles to feed and clothe me.

Then I remind them—while my mother might have resorted to fast food when she could get it and near starvation when she couldn't—I was always white. I had some measure of protection, even amidst poverty. These are hard things to admit. However, when a trusted professor gives her students testimony they can feel, students are ultimately empowered to embrace their own story, as well.

Hamilton: Moving from Feminist Theory to Practice

When I told my students I had a child with cancer, I changed from a feminist scholar into an engaged feminist teacher. This shift was greatly influenced by Hélène Cixous's (1976) *écriture féminine*. A contemporary rhetorician,

Cixous's body-rhetoric introduced feminism to *écriture féminine*, which articulates the connections between women's physical bodies and their experiences. In "The Laugh of the Medusa," Cixous reminds us that women have had to argue for the right to use language throughout history. So why had I insisted on teaching feminism but, at the same time, insisted on remaining silent about my experiences as a feminist?

In fact, I never shared anything about my personal life with students—not a word about my marriage, my toddler, and the ways my feminist pedagogy transferred into my life outside the classroom. Professors are supposed to be intellectuals who research all the time—they are not wives and mothers. Well, that is until my two-and-half-year-old daughter, Grace, was diagnosed with cancer.

When I wished students a happy Spring Break just days before Grace's diagnosis, I didn't mention my family's plan to travel to the beach, my concern that Grace had been sick off and on for weeks, nor did I ask them about their plans. So how was I to walk back into the classroom and explain to a room full of students that not only did I have a child that I never spoke of, but I would also be unable to continue as their professor because that child lay in a hospital bed three blocks away?

My head swam as I attempted to explain her diagnosis, prognosis, surgeries, and steroids, all of which were brand new to me, too. I was used to talking about the theory around women's and gender studies, social justice, writing and psychology, and now I found myself practicing it in front of a room full of teary-eyed undergraduate students.

From that day on, I was determined to be completely transparent with my students. I showed them Grace's medical website, where I wrote a blog about mothering a child with a life-threatening illness, organized service-learning activities with the Ronald McDonald House Charities, and told them about her chemotherapy schedule and friends of hers who lost their battles with cancer.

Based on my willingness to share, the conversations about writing and feminist theory and practice opened in ways I could never have imagined possible as a professor. About midway through the semester, I received affirmation that this was, in fact, a good pedagogical decision.

One of my students waited after class until we were the only two people left in the room: "I just wanted to say thank you. Thank you for coming back and for sharing Grace's story with us. My mom died of cancer several years ago, and people in my life, even close friends and family, avoid talking about her or cancer when I'm around. And that silence is so painful, so thanks for not doing that with us."

As Cathy Davidson (2017) reminds us, an engaged feminist pedagogy means we, as teachers, must acknowledge our relationship to power and share ourselves with students so that they can then share with the world, even when it means sharing that you have to miss a class because your child needs a blood transfusion.

A CALL TO ACTION

The embracing of one's own experiences fosters an open space where students feel validated in their difference and humbled in their commonalities. It is the admission of the teacher that she, too, can learn from her student. It is an honest and humble way of telling our students that we are in this together; our knowledge is both hampered and furthered by our experience, as is theirs. And that the sharing of ourselves with one another is how we see past those limitations and push forward together toward a greater understanding that surpasses and conquers them. And with that understanding comes a catalyst for change and action.

Personal stories provide insightful clarity when bland instruction and simple recitation of fact cannot. This chapter details the intimate stories of teachers, as they reconcile their personal experience with their professorial pedagogy. These anecdotes seek to address the need for finding common space through the sharing of experiences and the ways in which these lessons can positively impact a learning community.

Through open reflection on the impact of one's race, class, and gender, as well as the intersectional ways in which these oppressions and privileges coalesce together, teachers can provide their students with a better understanding of inequity.

CONCLUSION

Autobiography—and the accompanying vulnerability it holds—creates a safe space in which faculty and students alike can engage in risky academic behavior; creating and contributing together, bringing the personal to bear on the academic material, thus providing critical content and skills to be used within the classroom. This interaction creates more equitable, inclusive, and diverse forms of knowledge and experience, thus allowing the entire classroom community a more impactful educational journey.

Throughout this chapter, the authors have argued for "professors who embrace the challenge of self-actualization" while "providing [students] with ways of knowing that enhance their ways of knowing that enhance their capacity to live fully and deeply" (hooks, 1994, p. 22). Perhaps sharing our own

stories in the classroom is the best way to encourage this depth of transformative learning. What story will you share?

REFERENCES

Cixous, H. (1976). The laugh of the medusa. (Keith Cohen and Paula Cohen, Trans.).
    Signs, 1(4), 875–93.
Davidson, C. (2017). *The new education: How to revolutionize the university to pre-
    pare students for a world in flux.* New York: Hachette Book Group.
Freire, P. (1970). *Pedagogy of the oppressed.* New York: Continuum.
Harding, S. (1986). *The science question in feminism.* Ithaca, NY: Cornell University
    Press.
Harding, S. (1991). *Whose science? Whose knowledge? Thinking from women's lives.*
    Ithaca, NY: Cornell University Press.
Hill Collins, P. (2000). *Black feminist thought: Knowledge, consciousness, and the
    politics of empowerment* (2nd ed.). New York: Routledge.
hooks, b. (1994). *Teaching to transgress: Education as the practice of freedom.* New
    York: Routledge.
Rankine, C. (2016). The condition of black life is one of mourning. In J. Ward (Ed.),
    The Fire This Time (pp. 145–56). New York: Scribner.

Chapter Thirteen

We Are All in This Class: Digital Storytelling in the EDI Classroom

Alex Miller and Theo Calhoun

An equitable, inclusive classroom honors the diversity of its students and their experiences (Adams, 2016). However, in many classrooms, this diversity is often regarded as incidental to curricular content. Thus, while personal connections might be encouraged during class discussions, they are unlikely to appear anywhere on the final. This chapter challenges the binary that has historically placed scholarship and storytelling into two distinct categories by using digital storytelling as a scaffold to pursue the goals of equity, diversity, and inclusion (EDI) instruction.

It contends that the EDI classroom benefits from curricula that encourage students to situate their own stories within academic discourse and facilitates meaningful assessments that value student voice. In pursuit of this claim, this chapter will draw upon lessons learned during an ongoing initiative designed to incorporate digital storytelling into the Ethnic, Gender, and Labor Studies curriculum at the University of Washington Tacoma (UWT), an urban-serving institution that was recently recognized as being among the most ethnically diverse colleges in the nation.

Throughout, it will highlight the experiences of Theo Calhoun (they/them), an undergraduate student with a passion for activism, as they coordinated course content and personal experience while translating awareness into action.

ACTION-ORIENTED ASSESSMENTS

Creating inclusive classrooms that recognize and value the experiences of their students is an essential precondition to any EDI curriculum (Adams, 2016; Burrell Storms, 2012; Zúñiga, Nagda, and Sevig, 2002). However, this chapter argues that instructors interested in inspiring their students' movement from awareness to action would benefit from reevaluating the role personal narrative plays in facilitating this transition, particularly as it relates to assessment.

Effective praxis must include a consideration of how assessment synthesizes learning—how it shifts responsibility from instructor to student by inviting the latter to communicate what they have learned. In the EDI classroom, reflecting on the assessment phase of instruction is particularly important.

If the culminating learning objective driving EDI pedagogy is measured by "a student's preparedness and commitment to creating change and ending social injustice" (Hartwell et al., 2017, p. 144), assessment design needs to pursue these imperatives by requiring students to demonstrate their understanding through modes of communication that extend beyond the walls of the classroom to resonate in the real world.

UWT's digital scholarship initiative has found that, when implemented strategically, digital storytelling can catalyze this movement by providing students with meaningful assessment opportunities that celebrate their experiences and equip them with "the skills, resources, and coalitions needed to create lasting change" (Adams and Zúñiga, 2016, p. 97). Moreover, digital storytelling allows instructors to showcase their students' work in new and exciting ways, creating opportunities for both faculty collaboration and civically engaged scholarship.

However, arriving at these outcomes requires careful consideration of how best to structure formative learning experiences in order to prepare students for success. Because digital storytelling can necessitate a degree of vulnerability not typically required in traditional academic work, instructors must be intentional about cultivating classroom environments that encourage students to see themselves in the curriculum and to feel safe sharing these connections. Creating a context for this kind of exchange can be challenging, but the benefits of doing so are profound.

Reflecting on their experiences in courses that required them to consider their identity in relation to course content, student Theo observed that the vulnerability involved in this act "allowed me to engage with the material in a more meaningful way."

WE ARE ALL IN THIS CLASS

Foregrounding the relationship between course content and individual experience resides at the heart of the EDI classroom. Approaching instruction from this position does more than simply validate individual student voice; it makes social justice education relevant by allowing students to witness how oppression functions in the lives of others, which is an essential step toward fostering empathy and inspiring prosocial action (Adams, 2016; Adams and Zúñiga, 2016; Burrell Storms, 2012).

There are several activities EDI instructors can use early in a course to encourage students to think about themselves in relation to the curriculum. Conducting a "Privilege Walk" or discussing Peggy McIntosh's (1989) inventory of race-based advantages are both powerful ways to raise awareness while establishing knowledge that centers on student experience.

Theo's assessment of these activities speaks to their role in framing the urgency of EDI instruction: "It felt validating and refreshing to know that I was able to bring my many intersecting identities to the classroom. I was excited to see myself reflected in the class, and I felt like getting a sense of where everyone else was coming from really changed the way I understood the initial readings."

As Theo's comments indicate, the process of situating students within the EDI classroom occurs on two levels. On the one hand, students are *physically* encouraged to develop a sense of communal identity as members of a classroom environment founded on respect, empathy, and critical inquiry. On the other hand, students are invited to see themselves and their peers *conceptually* in relation to the systems of power and oppression explored within EDI-oriented course content.

Effective implementation of EDI instruction requires that teachers and students alike see themselves and their experiences resonate throughout the curriculum, for we all exist in relation to the systems of privilege and oppression that shape our lives. The remainder of this chapter will emphasize these connections while guiding readers through a sequence of scaffolding activities developed by faculty at UWT to lead students from their initial encounters with digital storytelling toward using the medium to take action and pursue real social change.

Step One: Introducing the Concept

Establishing a reciprocal relationship between students and curricula is an essential first step toward fostering EDI skills; however, inspiring students to pursue social change requires that instructors equip students with the skills needed to take action. Digital storytelling is uniquely suited to the task of transforming awareness and knowledge into action. Anyone who has ever seen a viral video understands the power of the digital medium. By layering image, audio, and text, digital compositions allow viewers to experience communication in a way that is nothing short of synesthetic.

The rhetorical opportunities afforded by the medium are myriad, and today's students often possess an innate understanding of their mechanics, even if they lack the terminology to describe what, exactly, they are witnessing. Digital media increasingly shares syllabus space alongside traditional texts, and this trend promises to continue as digital natives make the transition from students to teachers.

Instructors interested in incorporating digital storytelling into their EDI classrooms should begin introducing the concept of digital scholarship early and often. Doing so helps normalize and legitimate this unique brand of scholarship. An introductory online icebreaker activity that typically winds up revealing as much about individual students as it does about digital scholarship, in general, might ask students to share a social justice-oriented viral video that they have found to be particularly compelling. Upon sharing, students should also be required to view and respond to a peer's video.

In addition to providing instructors with a feel for their students' familiarity with issues related to course content, this low-stakes activity creates an archive of texts worthy of class discussion and allows students to get to know one another. Critiquing a selection of these videos in class is a great way to assess the rhetorical techniques that students can then emulate when they begin experimenting with their own digital stories.

Step Two: Introducing the Technology

After establishing the role that digital compositions can play in the EDI classroom, it is time to introduce the technologies that students will be expected to use while telling their stories. Here, instructors should remain mindful of obstacles to accessibility. Faculty at UWT have found that platforms such as WeVideo provide affordable, accessible alternatives to programs such as Final Cut Pro, which boasts both steep learning curves and prohibitive price tags.

When selecting a platform, instructors would be wise to consider student needs and err on the side of intuitive programs that allow collaboration and work across devices and operating systems. Time spent evaluating platforms prior to implementation is time saved once students begin experimenting.

Similarly, devoting instructional time to introducing the technology is equally important to ensuring student success. Although many of today's students may have come of age in an era of media supersaturation, instructors should not assume anything about their students' familiarity or comfort with producing media of their own. Moreover, while many students will greet this opportunity as a welcome change of pace from their typical coursework, others may require more convincing.

Thus, when introducing this component of the course, instructors should be sure to include an explanation as to *why* this activity is essential to achieving course goals as well as a detailed explanation as to *how* to use these technologies most effectively.

To assuage the anxieties that are often aroused when students are asked to think and communicate in unconventional ways, it is helpful to refer back to the introductory activity described above as evidence of how effective digital platforms can be at pursuing the learning objectives of EDI instruction. Students want their work to matter, and digital storytelling has the potential to affect audiences in ways that extend far beyond the reach of the traditional academic essay.

Instructors should also assure students that they will be given several opportunities to produce digital media through assignments that build and reward evidence of increasing proficiency with the technology instead of simply relying on a one-size-fits-all approach to assessing mastery. Adopting new technologies can be challenging for students and teachers alike; consequently, flexibility is a prerequisite for EDI courses that seek to include digital components.

Step Three: Calibrating Baselines

After introducing the technologies, instructors should allow students to experiment with the digital platforms the class will be using through low-stakes activities designed to increase their comfort with the mechanics of the medium gradually. A particularly effective early assignment might require students to work in pairs while creating a one-minute video log that invites them to introduce themselves while sharing their initial reactions to the course.

In addition to providing instructors with valuable insights as to how their students are negotiating course content, these short videos establish a baseline of technological proficiency that can later be used to assess growth as students progress toward their final projects. Moreover, by providing a venue where student voice is validated, these vlogs foreground the students' centrality within the EDI classroom.

Theo's assessment of these early activities confirms their importance as both an introduction to the technology and an opportunity for collaboration: "Starting with vlogs felt like an achievable task because it was kind of informal. I didn't feel intimidated—it was fun, and there was ample room for collaboration and troubleshooting with my peers. Being able to share tips and tricks, ask each other for help with tech issues, and learn from those around me was enjoyable, and it contributed to my success on the project."

As Theo's reflection indicates, low-stakes introductory activities are an excellent way to demystify this new mode of communication while creating a sense of class community.

Step Four: Amplifying Rigor

Having established a baseline, instructors should then introduce a second digital assignment that features increased expectations regarding the rigor of students' engagement with course concepts and familiarity with the digital platform. An activity that caters to both of these goals involves a new twist on a conventional assignment: the annotated bibliography.

In this iteration, students should conduct research and prepare annotations as they typically would; however, in addition to their written annotations, students should also be required to compose a digital translation of their work that communicates their growing expertise on a particular topic through a two-minute video. By emphasizing the concept of translation (as opposed to transcription), this activity is particularly effective in illustrating how shifting mediums require students to reconsider how best to present their information.

As this activity demands a bit more of students, it is helpful to devote instructional time to discuss how, exactly, written annotations evolve as they combine with images, video, and audio to create digital compositions.

Establishing low-stakes peer-evaluation cohorts is particularly useful throughout this activity, as they allow students to learn from their peers while identifying points of overlap in their research interests. Here, Theo's reflections on this phase of the larger project are instructive: "I appreciated that I had the ability to experiment throughout the quarter. Trying out different approaches, along with consistent feedback from Dr. Miller, allowed me to figure out what worked well and what didn't. This trial-and-error approach allowed me to become comfortable with the medium."

The activities discussed thus far present relatively novel approaches to introducing students to the digital humanities. Consequently, instructors need to be transparent regarding both the why and how that drives each of these assignments. Establishing rubrics that provide clear categories of assessment allows students to understand what, exactly, excellence looks like as they complete these unconventional tasks.

However, exemplars of outstanding student work are among the most effective means to communicate these goals. As instructors develop their own skills in teaching digital rhetoric, it is recommended that they amass a cache of student-generated works that can serve as teaching texts for students struggling to master these skills.

Step Five: Digital Activism

By scaffolding these introductory activities through comparatively low-stakes activities that encourage students to experiment with how best to communicate their learning on digital platforms, instructors have prepared their students to succeed while pursuing their final EDI learning objective: translating awareness and knowledge into actions that create change beyond the classroom.

Fortunately, transitioning toward this final goal represents more of a continuation of the work students have already been doing than a radical break from previous assignments. Here, having set aside instructional time to discuss the rhetorical power of viral videos pays dividends, as students should recognize the potential impact that their videos can have when disseminated broadly.

The final assignment should be designed to synthesize the learning that has occurred during the two introductory activities, both in terms of continuing to develop students' content mastery as well as further refining their digital acumen. Thus, instead of prompting students with a series of questions structured to guide them toward a uniform product, instructors should consider framing this assignment according to the core objectives that guide EDI instruction.

They will then challenge students to develop their own strategies for making their learning available to the general public and, in the process, inspiring change. Allowing students this degree of creative freedom requires a reciprocity of trust between student and teacher, but by agreeing to a set of general technical requirements and co-creating a rubric immediately after introducing the project, instructors and students alike can approach this assignment with confidence.

Having established the parameters of the assignment, students are now allowed to determine how best to tell their stories. To safeguard against final projects that fail to engage their audience, it is recommended that instructors check in on their students' progress through a series of formative assessments that build toward the final products.

Proposals, outlines, reflections, and scripts all allow students to map out the ideas driving their projects prior to beginning the digital composition phase, which is often too late in the process for feedback. Relying on the already-established cohorts to provide peer review is another effective way to maintain oversight.

CONCLUSION

In the spirit of EDI-driven instruction, final projects should be presented publicly in an event that is open to both campus and community. This should be more than a final class meeting; it should be a celebration of student learning that redirects the work of students outward to inspire others to feel passionate about issues of EDI. Instructors should encourage students to think of this occasion not simply as the conclusion of a course but as the beginning of something much larger. Reflecting on their experience during the class screening, Theo noted,

> After going through this process with my peers, seeing all the stories and scholarship come together was really powerful. Seeing everyone's final products and the accumulation of their research made my work in the class feel that much more valuable in a way that coursework doesn't often feel. Witnessing the impact of my project and its social-justice-oriented subject matter was empowering. My own openness about my identities presented in the project was beneficial both for myself and my peers to view. Viewing the work of my classmates and observing the vulnerability that they brought to their scholarship made me realize how much this class meant to us all. It just felt like we were all in the class.

Theo's final observation speaks to the potential digital storytelling has when employed within the EDI classroom. These digital stories are more than final projects; they represent a student's first step toward creating change in their world.

REFERENCES

Adams, M. (2016). Pedagogical foundations for social justice education. In M. Adams, L. A. Bell, D. J. Goodman, and K. Y. Joshi (Eds.), *Teaching for Diversity and Social Justice* (3rd ed.) (pp. 27–54). New York: Routledge.

Adams, M., and Zúñiga, X. (2016). Getting started: Core concepts for social justice education. In M. Adams, L. A. Bell, D. J. Goodman, and K. Y. Joshi (Eds.), *Teaching for Diversity and Social Justice* (3rd ed.) (pp. 95–129). New York: Routledge.

Burrell Storms, S. (2012). Preparing students for social action in a social justice education course: What works? *Equity and Excellence in Education*, 45(4), 547–60.

Hartwell, E. E., Cole, K., Donovan, S. K., Greene, R. L., Burrell Storms, S. L., and Williams, T. (2017). Breaking down silos: Teaching for equity, diversity, and inclusion across disciplines. *Humboldt Journal of Social Relations*, 39, 143–62.

McIntosh, P. (1989). White privilege: Unpacking the invisible knapsack. *Peace and Freedom Magazine* (July/August), 10–12.

Zuniga, X., Nagda, B. A., and Sevig, T. D. (2002). Intergroup dialogues: An educational model for cultivating engagement across differences. *Equity and Excellence in Education*, 35 (1), 7–17.

About the Authors

Jessica Baldizon is a teacher of English to speakers of other languages at a public elementary school in Connecticut. She serves as a service-learning coordinator and school-university partnership liaison. In the summer, she enjoys teaching writing labs for elementary and high school students with the CT Writing Project hosted at Fairfield University.

Nuala S. Boyle has supported the advancement of community-engaged teaching and learning in higher education since 1997. She is the inaugural (2010) director of the Center for Civic Engagement at Nazareth College in Rochester, NY, where she oversees curricular and co-curricular community engagement, including academic service learning, and she facilitates the college's experiential learning requirement in the core curriculum.

Stephanie L. Burrell Storms is an Associate Dean and Associate Professor of Multicultural Education at Fairfield University. Her research and scholarly interests include social justice education, scholarship of teaching and learning (SoTL), and faculty development. Stephanie is the Region 1 Director for the National Association for Multicultural Education.

Theo Calhoun is a recent graduate from the University of Washington Tacoma's School of Interdisciplinary Arts and Sciences, where they earned a degree in Ethnic, Gender, and Labor Studies.

Paul Carron is an Assistant Professor of Philosophy in the Baylor Interdisciplinary Core at Baylor University. He has published articles on Plato, Aristotle, and the primatologist Frans de Waal.

Kirsten Cole is an Associate Professor of Early Childhood Education in the Teacher Education Department at the Borough of Manhattan Community College, which is part of the City University of New York (CUNY) system. Her research interests include the study of teachers' lives, collaboration and mentoring in early childhood classrooms, and anti-oppressive education.

Ryan Colwell is an Assistant Professor of Childhood Education and Director of the Childhood Education Program in the Graduate School of Education and Allied Professions at Fairfield University. He previously served as a second and third-grade teacher in two Connecticut public school districts.

Sarah K. Donovan is a Professor of Philosophy at Wagner College in New York City. Her teaching and research interests include social, feminist, and community-engaged philosophy. She has taught in Wagner College's interdisciplinary and community-engaged programs since 2003.

Amy Eshleman, a Professor of Psychology at Wagner College, regularly teaches courses on gender, sexuality, race, and class in which she shares her research on expressions of prejudice with students. With Jean Halley, Eshleman co-authored *Seeing Straight: An Introduction to Gender and Sexual Privilege*, published by Rowman & Littlefield in 2017.

Victoria Felix is a counseling psychologist who teaches at Wagner College. She has authored multiple peer-reviewed journal articles.

Heather M. Finch is a higher-education professional with experience as an instructor, diversity and inclusion coordinator, mentor, and publicity representative. Her research focuses on how marginalized narratives of pre-nineteenth-century enslaved women are recovered and reimagined. Her teaching interests include perspectives on freedom and social justice.

Angela Fink is a Project Manager and Research Scientist for the Center of Integrative Research on Cognition, Learning, and Education (CIRCLE) at Washington University. Angela applies her empirical training to STEM education research, examining the cognitive, social, and motivational factors that influence college student learning and achievement.

Kristie A. Ford is a Professor of Sociology, Founder of the Intergroup Relations Program, and Director of the Center for Leadership, Teaching, and Learning (CLTL) at Skidmore College. Her research and teaching interests include: race and ethnicity, gender and sexuality, and social justice education. For her leadership in the field, she was named the Quadracci Chair in Social Responsibility in June 2019.

Regina (Gina) Frey is the Florence E. Moog Professor of STEM Education in Chemistry, and the Co-Director of the Center for Integrative Research on Cognition, Learning, and Education (CIRCLE) at Washington University. Gina was the head of The Teaching Center from 2001–2017, and she has expertise in STEM education research for higher education and faculty development.

Sarah Webster Goodwin is Professor of English Emerita at Skidmore College. She taught in the Intergroup Relations (IGR) Program from its inception at the college. Her research and teaching interests, in addition to subjects related to racial identity and IGR, include early nineteenth-century British literature, the history and cultural functions of sugar, and gender studies.

Ruth L. Greene is a Professor of Psychology and O'Herron Distinguished Professor at Johnson C. Smith University and a Faculty Affiliate of the UNC-Charlotte Urban Education Collaborative. Her teaching and research interests include educational, developmental psychology, and health and mental health disparities among African Americans.

Jean Halley is a Professor of Sociology and teaches at the College of Staten Island and the Graduate Center of the City University of New York (CUNY). Her books include *Boundaries of Touch: Parenting and Adult-Child Intimacy* (2007), *The Parallel Lives of Women and Cows: Meat Markets* (2012), and *Horse Crazy: Girls and the Lives of Horses* (2019).

Amy Hodges Hamilton is a Professor of English at Belmont University. Her research and teaching interests center on personal writing, feminist theory, trauma theory, and healing and the arts. Amy is most at home when writing and collaborating with students, which is evidenced in her most recent publication, "First Responders: A Pedagogy for Writing and Reading Trauma" in *Critical Trauma Studies* (NYU Press, 2016).

Erica Hartwell is an Associate Professor of Marriage and Family Therapy at Fairfield University and a licensed marriage and family therapist in the state of Connecticut. She teaches courses in social justice, couple therapy, research methods, therapist self-development, and LGBTQ issues. Her scholarship focuses on promoting social justice in mental health.

Natoya Haskins is an Associate Professor in the Counselor Education Department at the William & Mary School of Education. Her teaching centers on providing a collaborative educational experience that embraces culturally diverse perspectives and historical and contemporary social justice issues within school counseling and counselor education.

Cynthia Kerber Gowan has been teaching graduate courses in inclusive education at Nazareth College in the School of Education for over a decade. Kerber Gowan facilitates relationships and community-engaged learning opportunities between community agencies and other departments at Nazareth College through the LifePrep program.

Shelby Longard is an Associate Professor of Sociology at Belmont University. She has published on student-based social movements and grassroots organizing among LGBTQIA youth and is currently examining colorblind ideology and colorblind logic among students of color. Her teaching interests center on inequalities and social justice.

Charles McDaniel is Associate Professor in the Baylor Interdisciplinary Core and Church-State Studies. His most recent book is *Civil Society and the Reform of Finance: Taming Capital, Reclaiming Virtue.*

Alex Miller is a lecturer in the School of Interdisciplinary Arts and Sciences at the University of Washington Tacoma, where he teaches courses in Literature, American Studies, and Ethnic, Gender, and Labor Studies. His contribution to this collection is part of an ongoing project on the connection between affect and activism in digital scholarship.

Jacqueline Rodriguez is the Assistant Vice President for programs and professional learning at the American Association of Colleges for Teacher Education (AACTE), where she leads the content development for the association. Prior to her appointment with AACTE, Rodriguez was a faculty member in the School of Education at the College of William & Mary.

Ophelie Rowe-Allen is the Associate Dean and Director of Residence Life & Student Diversity and Multicultural Affairs at Fairfield University. During her thirteen years, she has worked to shift the cultural context to create a more diverse, inclusive, and equitable campus community.

Margarita Sánchez is a Professor of Spanish in the Modern Languages, Literatures, and Cultures Department at Wagner College. Her research interests include contemporary Latin American literature, with an emphasis on gender studies, and community-engaged scholarship with immigrant communities.

Erin Solomon is a Research Scientist and Project Manager for the Center of Integrative Research on Cognition, Learning, and Education (CIRCLE) at Washington University. She has worked on projects aimed at supporting STEM faculty as they implement evidence-based teaching strategies and collaborated with CIRCLE staff and faculty to conduct evaluation studies of these teaching strategies.

Theodora P. Williams is an Associate Professor Emerita of Human Resource Management at Marygrove College. She has designed and taught courses on diversity and inclusion for business professionals, business ethics, and human resource management. Her research interests include teaching with technology for improved learning outcomes and the scholarship of teaching and learning (SoTL). Her portfolio includes extensive work in accreditation for institutional effectiveness and compliance.